moving into balance

Creating your personal pathway

BARBARA LARRIVEE

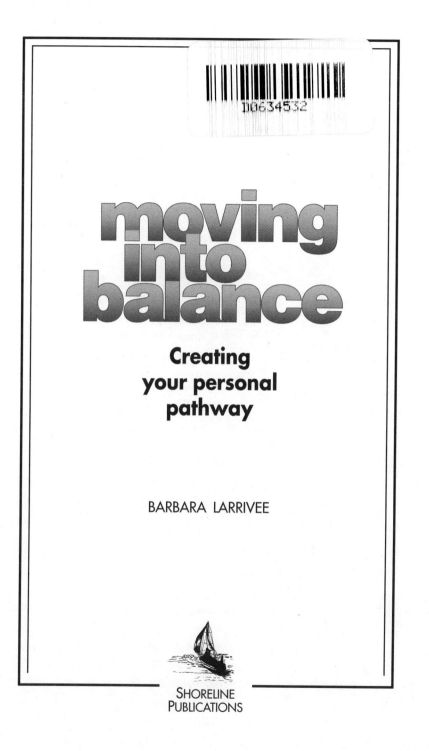

SHORELINE PUBLICATIONS

Printed in the United States of America

Design and production by White Light Publishing
Cover photo © 1996 PhotoDisc, Inc.

FIRST EDITION

Library of Congress Cataloging-in-Publication Data

Larrivee, Barbara.
    Moving into balance : creating your personal pathway / Barbara Larrivee. — 1st ed.
      p. cm.
    Includes bibliographical references.
    ISBN 0-9651780-9-9 (pbk.)
    1. Change (Psychology)   2. Self-actualization (Psychology)   3. Consciousness.
I. Title
BF637.C4L377 1996
158.1—dc20   96-92140
                                                    CIP

The author is grateful for permission to reprint: "Autobiography in Five Short Chapters" from *There's a Hole in My Sidewalk* copyright © 1993 by Portia Nelson. Reprinted by permission of Beyond Words Publishing, Inc.

*To all those struggling to bridge the gap between
doing and being, striving and letting go, effort and flow,
action and acceptance.*

Contents

Personal Exercises

Meditations

Diagrams

Personal Note

I am a member of a generation of avid self-help enthusiasts, now quite adept at continuously discovering what's wrong with themselves and others (especially parents and lovers) and following the latest prescriptions for fixing what's wrong. With the 90s as a backlash against continual self-improvement has come a new generation of self-help books, heralding *self-transformation*. This popular version of self-help endorses discovering our own inner wisdom, manifesting a state of bliss and tapping a higher self.

Because reading self-help books is a kind of modern-day addiction, I reasoned that if I was struggling to make sense of this new message, so were many others who were now reading these books. For many of us who have been working on ourselves over the years trying to become all that we believe we can be, the idea that it's time to stop practicing *how to be* and start *being* is very enticing.

For me, the passageway to arriving at this state of inner peace and bliss, to actualizing my higher self, was uncharted territory. This new approach seemed to describe a state of being, an end result, yet offered no map to guide the passage. I had a sense that I may have the tools but I wasn't sure how to tap them. While the arguments for abandoning traditional self-help strategies were quite compelling, and I could surely see the merits of being in this state of heightened consciousness, the gateway to this effortless odyssey which would reconfigure my way of seeing and being alluded me.

Many people are buying books and tapes that espouse both these competing perspectives on personal growth and are trying to use both with no means of finding the balance. How do we actualize our human potential? Is it through hard work and deliberate effort? Is it through creating a heightened consciousness? Is there a way to fuse these conflicting viewpoints for bringing about enduring change in our lives? Can we find the balance between a methodical change process and unleashing our naturally-flowing awareness?

Somewhere between here's exactly what to do, and there's nothing to do, lies the passage to bringing more peace and harmony into our lives and into our world. This book is for all those struggling to find the balance between letting it happen and making it happen.

Both perspectives have something to offer those attempting to strike a balance between flow and force. This book provides a clearer understanding of each perspective, offers ways to find one's personal balance drawing from each, and provides readers with a way to approach and implement desired changes in their lives.

In this book I share what I learned as I struggled to balance making a living and living a life. In this struggle, I gleaned some insights into the personal discovery process. I offer the story of my excursion as both guidance and affirmation. I write this book with the trust that the insights I have gained through my journey of self-discovery will benefit you in your quest to create harmony in your life and discover your pathway to moving into balance.

PART I

Creating Your Personal Pathway

The Examination Stage

Chapter 1

An Overview

This book is not a map with clear directions for getting from one point to another in the personal growth process. Rather, it is a journey of exploration, discovery, and reconciliation. I have organized this book into three parts which describe three major stages in the process of *moving into balance*: The Examination Stage, the Struggle Stage, and the Action Stage.

In Part 1, the Examination Stage, I begin with a description of the conflicting perspectives on personal growth: The interventionist *making it happen* perspective and the enlightenmentalist *letting it happen* perspective. Next, I lay out the process of moving into balance and offer the personal chronicle of my quest to move into balance to illustrate this process. In the final section, I present various viewpoints on personal growth, share how change has occurred in my life and challenge you to examine how change has occurred in your life.

Part 2, the Struggle Stage, is about the struggle to let go of our familiar ways of behaving. The struggle is really the struggle to learn to live as individuals in process, never finished products. In this section of the book I describe processes that act as *mediators* in the process of moving into balance. These processes are self-reflection, self-inquiry and self-talk. They serve as the vehicles for challenging our beliefs, assumptions, expectations, judgments, and actions.

The personal discovery journey is a lifelong journey, cycling through periods of confusion, uncertainty, conflict and chaos as we continuously discover new dimensions of ourselves and keep evolving. We need to grow more trusting of this necessary phase and come to know that our most important learnings emerge from the depths of inner turmoil and chaos. The process of moving into balance is a personal reconciliation where we come to know when the self-knowledge created through heightened awareness will be sufficient to bring about change in our lives, and when it will not suffice. Recognizing our blind spots and realizing we are stuck at the same point is part of the process of moving into balance. Sometimes we do need a specific strategy or intervention, a prescription for change. Our challenge is to find our own balance point between accepting what is and actualizing new ways of behaving.

Part 3, the Action Stage, contains the tools for moving into balance, staying in balance, and rebalancing when you find yourself moving off center. With the competing demands of everyday living, very seldom are we actually in balance. For most of us, the experience of balance comes in fleeting moments and is difficult to sustain. The idea is to hover close to the point of balance, catching yourself sooner and sooner as you start to move out of balance, becoming more aware of the warning signals alerting you that you need to rebalance. You move into balance when you are able to redefine and reposition your experiences so that you reinterpret the meaning of your experiences and begin to see things differently.

This section of the book offers practices and principles that keep us mindful of balance and keep us alert to the signs of imbalance. Because we are social beings, we are influenced and affected by relationships and interactions with others. So this part of the book also deals with our relationships with others and ways we can support others in their quest for balance in their lives. Our inner and outer worlds are reflections of each other. Just as our self-talk mediates our thinking process, what we say to others embodies our assumptions. It is not possible to be in balance without maintaining harmonious relationships with others. We stay in balance when we open our hearts and minds. Opening our hearts involves releasing ourselves from carrying resentments and judging others.

Chapter 2

Two Conflicting Perspectives

There are two distinct perspectives on personal growth. On the one hand, there are shelves of self-help books telling us to do this and don't do that, to constantly work on ourselves and our relationships, and to perpetually analyze our every action. On the other hand, the alternative perspective is that meaningful change is not brought about by trying to force change. It represents a complete turnaround, calling for a halt to all the doing and changing.

These conflicting perspectives on the pathway to personal fulfillment can be characterized as the "interventionist" perspective, advocating *making it happen* versus the "enlightenmentalist" perspective, endorsing *letting it happen.*

The Interventionist Perspective

The interventionists view change as a linear process, comprised of well-defined and sequential steps. A person makes a conscious effort to change and commits to a specified behavior change. The process is laborious, methodical and often painful. The interventionists advocate that the pathway to a more fulfilling life is a never-ending series of interventions entailing a lifelong commitment. The conviction is that you have to do the work before you can reap the benefits, the old "no pain, no gain" adage. Such interventions typically take the form of traditional individual, couple or group counseling, workshops that provide structured experiences and rely on personal insights gleaned through group process to effect change, multi-step programs implemented via the vehicle of a support group, or, for those do-it-yourselfers—the how-to self-help book.

The interventionist perspective takes the position that we have to "do our work" entailing a long-term commitment to indepth introspection involving working through much pain. The challenge confronting us is to face our fears head on, to deal with our denial and to take action to live our lives deliberately. Our task is to take control and change our destructive behaviors to more constructive behaviors by implementing a specific plan of action.

This popular approach to therapy and self-help has taken a mechanistic, problem-solving stance, reducing everything to its lowest common denominator. Complex issues are *solved* by reverting to a singular remedy characterized by how-to prescriptions. This prescriptive approach to self-help often offers a simplistic solution focusing on discreet behaviors with no vision of a more indepth transformational process. This approach has the advantage of keeping us focused on our goals and the potential limitation of promoting a tendency to become too self-absorbed and out of touch with our grander self. The concepts of health and well-being do not extend beyond personal boundaries to include the health of our community, our world, our planet and the well-being of our neighbors, both local and global.

The Enlightenmentalist Perspective

The enlightenmentalists herald awakening or enlightenment, a higher state, characterized by inner peace and bliss, viewing personal change as a self-transformative process. For the enlightenmentalists, there is no doing, no willing, no steps to follow. This avenue does not compel one to carry out any particular action plan. Its mission is to heighten consciousness and lead one to the realization of a higher self, embracing the inevitable ebb and flow of the journey toward self-fulfillment. The transformational process is not a pathway to follow, step by step, nor a journey to embark on, and eventually complete, but rather an effort-less odyssey, ultimately reconfiguring our way of seeing and profoundly altering our worldview.

The enlightenmentalist perspective advocates finding a means to expand your consciousness so that you begin to perceive things in a new light. This perceptual shift then allows you to tap an inner wisdom which opens up a window to self-knowledge. In this state of being, the pathway to change emerges by itself, with no overt effort.

The challenge facing those who embrace this approach is to live life consciously and mindfully, to bring their inner and outer worlds into bal-ance. This new challenge is to engage in the practice of daily conscious living. As we learn to become increasingly more and more aware we begin to open up to a greater range of choices.

Underlying both of these positions is still the idea that we need to change to bring more peace and harmony into our lives, and into our world. The interventionist approach to self-help often offers simple solu-tions without creating a more indepth understanding. On the other hand, the enlightenmentalist perspective advocates a state of being which is vir-tually impossible to sustain and fully function with the multiple demands of relationships, family and the workplace.

And yet, both perspectives have something to offer one attempting to strike a balance between flow and force, between letting it happen and making it happen. Both avenues have benefits and limitations. The inter-ventionist approach has the benefit of keeping us focused on our goals and a potential limitation of promoting a tendency to become too self-absorbed. Following someone else's path often obscures the emergence of our own path. On the other hand, the gateway to the emergence of self-knowledge is hard to access for most of us caught in the ongoing strug-gle to balance making a living with living a life. Our capacity to arrive at a blissful state comes in fleeting moments and is elusive.

This book is about defining a middle ground between taking charge and letting go. I open the gate and share my journey, but you must work your own way through the maze discovering your pathway to cre-ating balance in your life.

Chapter 3

Moving into Balance Flow

The process of moving into balance weaves us through a series of stages and phases. Although the process is actually more cyclical than linear or sequential, the diagram on page 11 provides a conceptual framework for explaining the process. The first stage is the *examination* stage. At this stage, we begin to notice our *ways of behaving* and start to *question* what a particular way of behaving is getting us. This behavior could be any behavior that we are bringing into question, such as getting angry, withdrawing, or working too much. At the next level we *challenge* whether our way of behaving is getting us what we want and explore the "cost" attached to our current way of behaving. When we move to the next phase, we have realized that our way of behaving is sustaining a state we want to change, such as discomfort, pain, unhappiness, or stress. This realization creates a surface or rational, understanding, leading to an expressed *desire for change*.

Attempting to let go of what is familiar creates a *struggle* and we find ourselves in *conflict*. This begins a critical stage in the moving into balance flow. If this state of *inner turmoil* brings about too much fear and doubt, we may close down the process and either stay with the old way of behaving or seek a quick fix. We look for a ready-made solution, a "prescription" for change. However, when we do this, we circumvent a whole loop in the personal discovery process. If instead we are able to face the conflict, *surrendering* what is familiar, we allow ourselves to experience the *uncertainty*. This not knowing throws us into *chaos*. At this point, if we move into the eye of the storm, riding the crest of the waves of chaos, we "weather" the turmoil and a deeper understanding emerges, moving us to the *reconciling* phase. At this phase, we have had a shift in our way of thinking, sensing and being. We have had a clearing and are seeing things in a new light, allowing us to create a vision of what we need to do.

In the final stage, the *action* stage, we set this vision into operation, *actualizing new ways of being.* At this stage we engage in new patterns of thinking and may implement new strategies, techniques, tools and skills to begin acting in ways more likely to satisfy our needs and fulfill our aspirations. We *move into balance* as we weave in and out of our old and new ways, having created an internal sense of when we need to control and when we need to surrender to respond appropriately to life's situations and circumstances.

If we complete the cycle, moving through the struggle, then we have experienced a transformation rather than a mere change in behavior. It is facing the turmoil, the conflict, the uncertainty, and the chaos that allows us to transcend a singular behavior change to unveil a window to self-knowledge. This shift restructures our way of seeing and changes our worldview.

Moving into Balance Flow

STAGE 1 Examination	Way of Behaving
	Questioning
	Challenging
	Desire for Change
STAGE 2 Struggle	Inner Turmoil / Conflict
	Surrender
	Chaos / Uncertainty
	Reconciling
STAGE 3 Action	Actualizing New Way of Being
	Balance

A Personal Chronicle of the Quest to Move into Balance

My quest to balance the old and the emerging belief moved through a number of phases. First came a questioning of the old belief that had served as a driving force for many years. This belief, the belief that personal growth meant never-ending "work," no longer seemed to fit. As I continued my exposure to what advocates of *enlightenment* were offering, through reading, listening to tapes, and attending workshops and lectures, my old belief began to shift. The next phase involved an intellectual understanding and advocacy for the emerging belief that growth was an "unfolding," a much less deliberate effort than "working" to change. As I moved to the next phase, I was beginning to grapple with the conflict that came with the abandonment of a familiar position. It was the struggle to create a pathway to actualizing this "unfolding." The next phase was my coming to grips with the fears and doubts brought on by the chaos I had been tossed into by letting go of what was familiar. It was my attempting to answer the question "How am I to be?". It played out as an inner struggle of control and surrender. The final phase was the ahah! stage where it finally came to me that having the new belief did not end the struggle, rather it created a new and different struggle; it redefined the struggle. This was my process of reconciliation—the process of moving into balance.

Examining the Old Belief: Growth as Work

In my own journey, I had traveled the *interventionist* path, extending great effort "working on" myself, working very hard at becoming self-actualized and self-reflective. In my personal voyage toward a more meaningful existence I had successively embraced a myriad of interventions and read a plethora of self-help books. And I willingly shared all the insights I gleaned with others. I had actually become a sort of "self-help connoisseur." I had read all the books, knew the best ones and could actually prescribe just the right one to solve any problem. I knew who needed a "light bouquet" and who would be better served by a "full-bodied" variety. It was so easy then—problem/solution—end of story!

Emerging Belief: Growth as Unfolding

As I truly believed the process of personal growth to be an endless process, I diligently continued to seek out the latest and most celebrated self-help books. Alas, the key to reaching my human potential had undergone a metamorphosis. The latest version of self-help books were no longer depicting the personal growth process as drudgery, but as effortless. Had we really come full circle? I had only to visualize and believe for wealth and bliss to be mine. Finally, there was no more doing, only being. I was ripe for this transformation. I had paid my dues, hadn't I?

I was beginning to tire of working on myself and was thinking I was about ready to rest on my laurels. After all, I had learned how to listen empathetically, share my true feelings, convert my self-defeating self-talk to self-affirming self-talk, and get the love I really wanted. I had embraced my inner child, befriended the warrior within, ran with the wolves, and abandoned judgment in favor of acceptance. I had reclaimed myself, taken charge and made it happen. Could there really be more work to do? The metaphor of growth as work was wearing me down. I would rather just unfold graciously, like a flower.

When I let go of who I am, I become what I might be.

—LAO TZU

Conflict Between the Old and Emerging Beliefs

In this new space I found myself in, this vision of unfolding resonated well. I had worked on myself with abandon, and everyone else in my life space. Enough already—amen!

And yet, while my intellect was saying "ahah," "now I see," "oh, yes, I am enlightened," "I have awakened," I seemed not to be able to translate these emerging beliefs into daily practice. The transformation was in words only, the integration into life form was not forthcoming. I was trying to think bliss, but I was living stress. I was perplexed. I just didn't get it. I was clueless. I had no plan.

All 'graduations' in human development mean the
abandonment of a familiar position...
all growth...must come to terms with this fact.
—ERIK H. ERIKSON

I was jarred by this new notion of not trying to force things to happen. I had mastered the art of making things happen. I always had a plan, a beginning, an end and was quite successful in my pursuits. I reasoned that not trying to make things happen meant not having a plan, not directly working toward something. But when I abandoned my plan nothing happened. Something was wrong here. I had trusted the flow of the universe to take me where I wanted to go, but I was stuck.

This inner conflict sparked my further exploration to try to reconcile what on the surface appeared to be opposing perspectives—effort versus flow, intentionality versus spontaneity, being in control versus relinquishing control, making it happen versus letting it be.

It is good to have an end to journey toward; but it is
the journey that matters, in the end.
—URSULA K. LE GUIN

Struggle to Reconcile the Old and Emerging Beliefs

The struggle between making it happen and letting it happen surfaced for me as I began writing this book. I had already written several books, so the writing process was familiar. I had a writing style that was productive for me. The style that I was comfortable with was to thoroughly exhaust a topic by amassing whatever information was available. I was quite compulsive about conducting a total exploration of the topic, uncovering everything that had been written. I would accumulate reams of notes and perseverate in ordering and reordering them before I felt ready to write. This was indeed a tedious process.

As I started to write this book, I found myself "caught in the middle" right inbetween *having* to make it happen and *wanting* to let it happen. My old brain wanted to keep collecting and organizing more and more notes, do what was familiar. Now the emerging me was trying to incorporate my new ideas about letting things proceed in a natural flow. My way of translating this new thinking was that I should not try to force myself to write, that writing should flow naturally because I was giving up my effort to control.

As you could probably guess, when I tried to just let words flow, the well was dry. When I tried to write without reference to my notes, thinking this was a more "natural way" of writing, my writing was simplistic and the complex nature of the concepts did not come through. Here I was, caught in the middle.

Because I thought I had made writing too tedious a process, integrating and synthesizing copious notes to formulate new understandings, I was trying to *force* a new writing style. In the process of reconciling force versus flow what I learned was that I couldn't force a writing style that was not my own. And yet, there was force involved. I did have to force myself to sit and write. There was conscious control involved to keep me working at it. What my emerging ideas about letting go contributed was stopping the self-recriminations about being in the wrong space. I needed to accept what it took for me to get the job done right now. If I was going to get this book written I had to do what was familiar. It may not be my ideal of what was a naturally-flowing process, but it was what worked for me.

This was my first glimpse of the reconciling process I wanted to write about—that delicate balance between acceptance and action.

Actualizing the Emerging Belief and
Moving into Balance

When I began writing this book, I believed I had something to share that had not been written about. It had to do with personal discovery and transformation, but I was struggling with exactly what form it would take. I thought I had to have it down perfectly before I could write. I was assuming that I had to figure it out first. Then I would be able to tell *the* truth. After all, I was part of a generation of women who not only thought they had to do everything but had to do everything better than it had been done before. We had to be perfect and we weren't settling for anything short of perfection! We just kept trucking trying to get it all right. (Fortunately, most of us have given up that quest!)

Finally, after many false starts and much self-condemnation, it came to me. What a revelation. I realized it was the turmoil, the conflict, the process of figuring it out that was the important story to tell. Along the way, there were important insights, significant realizations, and painful lessons worth sharing, but the essence was the reflective process itself. What was worth sharing was the process of reconciling this inner struggle, the process of moving into balance.

Chapter 4

The Personal Growth Process

I began to question the notion of intervention, both in terms of my own personal growth path as well as in my work. What I was questioning was the whole notion of whether people actually changed their behavior through the process of implementing specific interventions. I am defining an intervention as any overt attempt to systematically change behavior, typically taking the form of a strategy, technique or series of steps designed to alter a specific behavior. It could be other-directed or self-directed, pre-packaged or self-designed. The process typically involves a variety of active practice techniques along with some way to monitor the change to evaluate progress. Active practice techniques are specific strategies to overtly practice new ways of acting and reacting, often coupled with explicit self-prompting or cueing strategies.

I was questioning the concept of intervention relative to my own personal growth as I continued to read self-help books and attend workshops. The ideas presented seemed meaningful at the time and while I was immersed in the workshop or book I was convinced I would follow the steps recommended to address a particular area of concern in my life. Somehow I never got around to actually implementing the steps, and yet there were always things that stuck, even without following the program or "doing the work."

Those who devise prescriptive programs of action do so with their unique framework for organizing theories and information. Then they present their organizational framework as if it represents the way things *are* when, in fact, it merely represents *their reality*, the way they have organized their world in order to make sense of it. While under the influence of their perspective we are believing their reality, but as soon as we get away from the program our own way of seeing and being reestablishes itself making it difficult to follow someone else's prescriptions.

Here was an important recognition for me. As I began to reflect on my personal growth path, it occurred to me that what I was advocating in my writing and in my work was not congruent with my own personal growth process. That is, I had not systematically followed a particular program of action, a preplanned agenda, or a series of sequential steps. And yet my behavior had changed dramatically over the years. Clearly, I had benefited, moved, shifted and changed in ways that significantly enhanced the quality of my life. There was a conscious intention to change but it seemed not to be in the form of a specific intervention, or systematically following someone else's prescribed plan.

To illustrate, I'll describe my coming to use active listening in place of telling or giving solutions. By active listening I mean empathic listening, or going beyond the spoken words to the, often unspoken, underlying emotions. The term connotes a way of listening in which the listener is an active partner, clarifying perceptions (or misperceptions) and acknowledging and verbalizing the feelings that may or may not have been said.

I was not specifically taught active listening in a class or workshop. I read about active listening and became an advocate. Over time I came to use active listening quite effectively. In analyzing how I have tried to teach active listening, I realized it had been through a tedious process; going from recognizing the benefits, to practicing by writing examples, to getting feedback on accuracy, to doing self-correction, and so on and so forth.

Now did I learn to use active listening through such a process? The answer is no. I never overtly practiced. Instead, over time I became aware of what happened when I failed to actively listen as compared to what happened when I was an active listener. Gradually, my behavior changed. Why did it change? It changed because my belief system had actually changed. I used to view myself as the expert. I had all this knowledge that I needed to impart to those less learned. And so, I didn't listen, I told. I didn't facilitate others in their own process of problem resolution, I diagnosed and prescribed.

Gradually, I challenged my belief that I was a fountain of knowledge and began instead to believe that truly significant learnings somehow surfaced from within. People change through a personal discovery process, subsequently formulating new behaviors that lie within their comfort zone and are aligned with their own styles of relating. As my belief changed, my role no longer was to impart knowledge but to somehow eke it out, coax it by providing a nurturing and supporting climate for self-knowledge to emerge.

Imagine what havoc this new realization caused for me! I had been trained in the behavioral model of breaking things down to their most basic level and teaching each discreet component as if it were an entity unto itself. This basic skill mastery model is one of skill building through cumulative practice of successively more and more difficult applications. This model represents a very different paradigm for learning than creating a context for self-knowledge to emerge. This line of thinking is also common to many therapeutic approaches advocating taking "baby steps" when attempting to change a self-defeating behavior. Practicing confronting behaviors in "safe" settings and then moving progressively on to more and more difficult situations is an example of this approach.

As I continued to think about this, I became aware that I had integrated active listening into daily practice not because I thought it was good or right but because I really did want to hear what others were saying and feeling. Why was this important to me? It was important because it connected me on a deeper level with those I cared about. I also reaped personal benefits because often the insights others had into their own actions sparked my own insights. When I was able to really listen with an openness that allowed me to be the mirror of self-reflection for another person, I felt gratified. I had come to realize the importance in my life both of having supportive relationships and being supportive in relationships. I chose to prioritize sustaining such relationships by consciously reallocating my time to allow for the nurturing of these relationships.

This recognition was quite enlightening because I realized that in my work I had been operating on the premise of the inherent goodness of active listening. It was so obvious to me that it was better than the alternatives, telling or not listening. It became apparent why others frequently were disinterested in learning these strategies — they really didn't value hearing and knowing the feelings of others. The result was not worth the effort. In fact, it often got in the way of getting the job done expediently. The idea is that personal meaningfulness is what drives change. Change is not an event, but a process.

Change occurs in the process of internalizing a belief.

—B. L.

∽

As I continued to try to make sense of the dilemma, I began to think that perhaps what I was really struggling with was an integration process. Until my new beliefs are transformed into practice at an automatic level, I have to make a conscious effort to change. When this transformation finally occurs, I behave in the desired way without conscious effort. That is, as a result of a very conscious and deliberate effort trying to do certain things and not to do other things in my life, I arrive at the point of not having to try—the doing has become automatic. This occurs as a consequence of actually changing my belief system by reprogramming old patterns of behaving. I'm still doing but the doing has become fully integrated so that it is now a way of being. In essence, what had been a conscious struggle to change behavior, is now a natural way of behaving.

A personal example is my moving away from automatically feeling hurt and closing down when I was criticized or my needs were ignored. My way of protecting myself was to shut down and pout and "not talk" for days. This way of acting was my attempt both not to yell and accuse which was what I had seen my parents do, and to punish for not getting what I wanted by withdrawing attention and affection. Gradually, as I learned to accept ownership for my feelings, my automatic response actually shifted to one of self-examination. Instead of asking "Why *did* he do this to me?" or worse, "How *could* he do this to me?" I now ask "What is *really* causing my hurt?" and more importantly, "What can *I* do? Is there something I need to ask for?" My need to blame and punish has nearly vanished.

Next, I tried to apply this line of thinking to the concept of control and the polarities of being in control versus relinquishing control. My basic beliefs about control have undergone a drastic change. Having been trained in the behavioral model of reinforcement theory, I used to believe that behavior was controlled by external reinforcement. The theory is quite simple—people tend to do things they get rewarded for and not do things they get punished for; behavior is controlled by external stimuli, or reactions *to* behavior. Adhering to this theory leads us to try to manipulate the behavior of others by dispensing rewards and delivering punishments. Punishing others typically only suppresses their behavior temporarily, it doesn't change behavior. Another side effect of using punishment is that it often leads others to want to escape and avoid the person delivering the punishment, or to a desire for revenge or retaliation against the punisher.

Now I believe that, try as I may, I can really only control my own behavior. And, I don't have the power or the right to control the behavior of others. (Nor do I want the responsibility!) I also don't want to let others control my actions. I believe control to be an inner action governed by my own internal thought process and mediated by my inner speech, or self-talk. So the way we exercise control is to monitor and regulate what we think and what we tell ourselves. Clearly, this is a very different way of perceiving control. My shift in thinking has evolved over many years.

Although I have let go of my desire to control others and my need to be in control of everything, this is not to say that I don't still find myself on occasion trying to control others. But I now have an internal alarm that goes off allowing me to see my controlling behavior and recognize it for what it is. As a consequence of continuous self-reflection, at times my reflection is automatic, allowing me to see what is happening without cueing myself to actively reflect on my behavior. While most of the time my behavior is consistent with my belief and there is no effort involved, as soon as I am aware of inconsistent behavior, there is a conscious and deliberate effort to change to behavior congruent with my non-controlling belief. By continually "holding up the mirror" and "viewing" our actions we learn to look to ourselves rather than to others to evaluate our behavior choices. This is the essence of reflective practice.

Reflections on Change

Following Your Own Path

I'm intrigued by the popular allusion to life's path or journey. The idea is that we are each on our own path. Now consider what it means to say a person is on his or her own path. Does being on your own path mean that one's path is predetermined? Does being on your own path mean that you create your own path by the choices you make (sort of the notion you made your bed, now sleep in it)? Does being on your own path mean that it's the journey itself, not actually the pathway to somewhere, that is the essence of life? Does being on your own path mean that it's not your life experiences per se but how you respond to them that defines your quality of life? Is following your own path merely tantamount to doing your own thing? Or, is following your own path just a metaphor for life being a unique journey for each of us? Is there an implicit assumption that we should not try to intervene in the lives of others, not try to alter their paths? Is the key the idea that one's path *is* one's path and we need to accept that there are many paths in life and not judge our path to be better, or someone else's path to be worse?

Change is Loss

Thinking about life's paths rekindles my thoughts about change. We do know some things about change. We know change is inevitable. We also know that people tend to be resistant to change. Change is often difficult. Change often seems to come at the very worst time. But we also know change is necessary. With change comes loss. There's something left behind when we move on.

What Makes a Person Ready to Change?

It is a mystery as to why and when one is ready to embrace a belief, hear a notion or see a perspective. Why do some people stay stuck in self-defeating behaviors while others are able to change to more need-satisfying behaviors? Why does one person merely understand a particular notion while another person attributes deep meaning and benefits in a profound way? Why is it that some stay at the cognitive level while others are prompted to action?

Timing and fit are both factors which can effect whether a person is ready or open to change at any point in time. The timing component represents a readiness to look at a particular aspect of one's life. If a person is involved in a crisis in another area of life, a relationship crisis or a work problem, the person may not be ready to put energy into personal growth issues. The fit component is the immediate connection or spark that the idea gives off. For some reason the inner eye sees that an important nerve has been touched.

The change process is elusive in the sense that we cannot predict the level of impact a particular idea will have on a person, or when a new understanding will be an awakening. What may appear to be a very simple recognition can sometimes have a far-reaching impact. For example, take the simple notion that you need to ask for what you want. While the idea is quite simple, if you have been holding onto the belief that you *should* get what you need and want without having to ask for it, the relearning that will be involved to operationalize this belief in your daily living is immense. A friend related a story of the early days of her marriage. On her birthday, her husband would just get her a card. Growing up in her family a birthday was an occasion for an all-out celebration. In his family, money was scarce and birthdays were not celebrated. So she wanted a big bash and he thought a card was enough. After a few years of getting furious, she finally told him what she expected on her birthday. She told him she wanted to go out to dinner, have a birthday cake, and get presents. When he knew what she was expecting, he had no problem giving her what she wanted. Her reaction was likely tied to the belief that "If someone loves you, he *should* know how to make you happy. This type of "fairy tale" thinking is the demise of many a relationship.

While you may be able to say, "Oh yes, it makes sense that I need to ask for what I want," in order to begin actualizing this belief you may have to challenge highly ingrained ways of behaving. But, if you are able to ask for something rather than relent that no one noticed you needed something, it can have a significant impact on your level of contentment. On the other hand, you may be able to immediately act on this notion upon being presented with it if you do not have any counter beliefs that need to be reprogrammed before you can take action.

Change as Continuum

Although change can sometimes be spontaneous and dynamic, it can also be more incremental or gradual. Change can be thought of as progressing along a continuum, influenced by many factors such as our history, experiences, awareness, understanding, motivation, effort, and so on. These factors all impact how far we are able to move on the continuum from less effective to more effective ways of perceiving, acting and reacting.

Ironically, it is often those who might benefit the most from changing their behavior who are the least likely to change. Those who have the farthest to move on the continuum are sometimes the most resistant to change. Movement at the beginning of the continuum can often be more difficult than movement near the end of the continuum. That is to say, it is easier to go from good to better than it is to go from bad to slightly better. It seems that those who are closer to the positive end have the greatest potential to move forward. These are the people who are reflecting on their behavior, seeking understanding and striving for self-knowledge.

A journey of 1000 miles must begin with a single step.

—LAO TZU

Although the change process can be incremental, change often comes in spurts. At points in the change process we may reach an awareness level which propels us forward. Conversely, we may get stuck somewhere along the continuum and not be able to go any further; we may even regress. Our progress may be stunted only until we work through an unresolved issue or conflict, or it may be permanently halted. We all have certain self-defeating behaviors that we are able to make some progress on, but there will be a limit as to how far we can go.

Change and Overgeneralizing

Another phenomenon which can be operating regarding change is a tendency to overgeneralize, or to tack on some extension to the new learning that is erroneous. This can result in rendering a desirable new behavior both productive and counterproductive. An example for me came early in my personal growth path. It involved the concept of accepting personal responsibility for my feelings, changing the belief that other people or situations cause me to feel and act in certain ways, to the belief that I am responsible for my own thoughts, feelings and behavior. This learning occurred as a result of attending workshops and seeking counseling to try to work out marital problems. I can remember trying very diligently to eliminate from my vocabulary phrases like "you make me feel..." and to replace them with "I feel..." statements.

I was caught up in believing what was in all the fairy tales—you find your "prince charming" and you live happily ever after. Why wasn't my prince charming meeting my every need and *making* me happy? I had to learn that my most important relationship was with myself. It was up to me to create happiness.

Learning to accept responsibility for my own feelings helped me to look at my own hurt and accept my anger and my disappointment. This represented a significant move forward and was the beginning of my abandonment of blame and judgment.

However, I began to realize that the way I had internalized this new belief was that I am responsible for my own feelings, therefore, I have to deal with them by myself, on my own. Entangled in this belief was the idea that others should not be held accountable (even made aware of!) their behavior that resulted in my feeling bad. I also held the conviction that others were not so "enlightened" rendering me responsible for not making others feel bad, because they don't know that they are responsible for their own feelings. What I seemed to be doing was trying to protect the other person at the expense of swallowing my own hurt, then disregarding or denying the consequent resentment of that person. Somehow embedded in this new belief that I was responsible for my own feelings was the idea that I don't have the right to have negative feelings toward another person. My thinking went like this: If I am responsible for my own feelings then I don't have the right to blame another person. If I relinquish them from any responsibility, then I can't get angry with them. Now, if I'm not allowed to be angry at another person then I'll have to be angry at myself for being too sensitive. Now, of course, the appropriate message was that if I am responsible for my own feelings, so are others responsible for their own feelings. Accepting responsibility for my own feelings did not preclude my sharing my feelings with others.

While this was the beginning of my self-reflective behavior and my attempt to move away from blaming others, I still had a lot of unpacking to do to begin to define the limits of my responsibility and to accept my right to stand up for myself and to have and express negative feelings of disappointment, frustration, hurt, and anger. This step was a very important step for me to begin to go inside rather than outside to make sense of my feelings and to see that the behavior of others was just their best attempt at the time to satisfy their needs, not behavior directed toward me. But at the same time, the overextended meaning which I attached to this new belief resulted in a new set of assumptions which I then had to challenge. The process of disputing these irrational notions took several more years.

What Does it Take to Change?

Thinking about change in terms of personal growth raises a host of questions. The foremost of which is why some people stay stuck in their ineffective behavior patterns while others are able to change to more effective behaviors. Especially perplexing are those people who are continually exposed to personal growth opportunities but manage not to grow at all. We all know people who always have a new explanation for why they are the way they are, but for them this realization serves merely as an excuse to continue behaving in the same way. The discovery does not lead to a change in their way of behaving.

Freud believed that the display of something often signified its lack. Those who always talk about how much they have gained from their personal insights have probably not grown much at all. In the same vein, those who tout sensitivity are often the least sensitive to the feelings of others. Those who are very quick to say "I'm sensitive" are typically masters of instilling guilt in others. "Now see what you've done, you made me feel bad." You become responsible for their feelings, yet they feel no responsibility to consider your feelings in their retaliation for feeling hurt. They are unaware that their own behavior is insensitive, exactly the behavior they are rebelling against. Identifying themselves as sensitive is their defense for considering only their own feelings. Their outward behavior of being sensitive is in actuality a disguise for the lack of sensitivity.

What does it take to bring about a change? It seems that for some it takes nothing less than a life-threatening experience. Somehow facing immanent death is an all-awakening experience for some and they change profoundly. For some people it is attendance at a packaged self-help program (e.g., AA, Al-Anon, The Forum, Lifespring, Avatar, A Course in Miracles) that provides the impetus for change to occur. For others, it is the connection with a religious or spiritual movement. But for the majority of us, change is a much more elusive quest.

PERSONAL EXERCISE

Gaining Insight Into Change in Your Life

Try this exercise to gain insight into how change has occurred in your personal growth journey.

1. Think about the changes—ways of behaving, thinking, relating— that have enhanced your life.

2. Make a list of changes you "paid for" or deliberately sought. These are the changes you can attribute to training you received, therapy, a program or workshop, a book you read, and so forth.

3. Next, make a list of the things you've "come to know." These are the changes that have occurred over time where you can't quite say what lead to the change.

4. From your two lists of changes, which ones have you fully-integrated into your daily practice? That is, which ones do you follow without having to remind yourself?

5. From your two lists of changes, which ones require constant revisiting? That is, you seem to "know" them, but honoring them requires a constant relearning.

Questions for Self-reflection:

• Have your important changes been changes in behavior or changes in the meaning of your experiences? Often important changes are not changes in actual behavior, rather they are changes in the meaning of your experiences; that is how you interpret your experiences.

In a recent workshop, some of the "paid for" changes listed were:

- Patience and discipline gleaned from years of Karate lessons
- "You can't push the river" learned from studying the Taoist teachings
- Staying present learned from Jungian psychology studied to become a therapist

Some of the "come to know" things listed were:

- I don't need to have everyone like me.
- I'm allowed to make mistakes.
- Others don't get to judge how I should feel.
- You have to ask for what you want.
- It's okay to say no.
- What you do is not as important as how you do it.

Those fully-integrated into daily practice:

- I don't need to have everyone like me.
- I'm allowed to make mistakes.
- Others don't get to judge how I should feel.

Those requiring constant revisiting:

- You have to ask for what you want.
- It's okay to say no.
- What you do is not as important as how you do it.

It's easy to become engulfed in the daily pressures of living and loose track of the important lessons you have learned. Integral to the moving into balance process is finding a way to remind yourself of what you already *know*.

There is a saying that there are no mistakes, only lessons to be learned. And a lesson is repeated until learned. The lesson will present itself in various forms until you learn it.

Change as Perceptual Shift

Individuals who cope successfully with stressful situations hold basic attitudes toward life. Susan Kobasa, a psychologist who studied "stress hardiness" labeled these attitudes the three Cs: Challenge, commitment, and control. The stress-hardy person interprets crises as challenges, adventures, opportunities to grow and learn. These people have a sense of meaning in life, a commitment to a higher sense of order in the universe, allowing them to see events within this larger perspective. They also have a sense that they have some kind of control over their lives, an empowerment to make a difference.

Those who experience stress differ from those who don't have stress primarily on the basis of their self-talk. Hermann Witte, a researcher in stress management, categorized these two broad types of people as either "thick-skinned" or "thin-skinned." For "thin-skinned" people, their habitual self-talk leads them to overreact to inner and outer events and stress themselves. For "thick-skinned" people, their habitual self-talk leads them to a much more balanced reaction to potential stressors.

In a recent study undertaken to identify characteristics which sustain health, Ronald Pelletier, a pioneer physician in the mind-body connection, found similar traits. In examining 53 case studies, some of the characteristics which emerged included having a sense of purposefulness to their lives which went beyond individual goals, having a way to create silence by going inside to a place of inner peace, and having the courage of their convictions, allowing them to make choices in their lives which were counter to conventional wisdom.

These examples of research suggest that those successful at managing stress and sustaining health embrace an empowering belief system, embodied by a way of thinking which creates a balance in the face of potential stressful situations, and an inner sense of life's purposefulness.

While knowing the traits that sustain a perspective that enhances one's life does help us explain why some individuals seem to be more proficient at life, it doesn't tell us how to bring about these traits when they are lacking. The mere knowing that these traits exist does not mean that we then know how to instill these traits. This knowledge doesn't readily translate into specific prescriptions for change.

The question is, if a person lacks these desirable traits, can we define a process that will enable one to acquire them? How does one come to reinterpret crisis from punishment to be endured to challenge to grow from? How does one shift a sense of powerlessness to a sense of empowerment? How does one expand one's vision beyond self to embody a higher self? How do we make the transformation from living by other's expectations to living by our own inner convictions? We know people make such perceptual shifts but can we prescribe a method for such transformations? How can we be guided to see what we don't see? How can we be awakened to see our true self, to break through the barrier of the assumed self?

Fragmentation Versus Interconnectedness

Studying those who have been "successful" by some generally-accepted definition of success related to the field of study is a common design for conducting research. The purpose is to then isolate characteristics that appear to be common. The implicit assumption of this type of research is that if we can identify characteristic traits, then we can teach others to acquire these traits. In education, we study proficient readers to identify strategies they use in the reading process to try to inform the practice of teaching less proficient readers. Some have attempted to decipher the complex thinking process which drives problem-solving and decision-making in the classroom setting. The resulting research findings are then translated into strategies to be used in the training of new teachers.

However, while this line of research enhances our understanding of the complex nature of any action, it has largely failed to bring about the expected results inasmuch as there is not a direct link between the identification of characteristics of proficient performers and the transmittal of these characteristics to less proficient performers. This is because when we try to isolate factors we lose the web that defines the connectedness of the isolated factor. We operate under the erroneous assumption that these factors can be added together to form the whole.

This orientation to isolate and thereby fragment characterizes the way we teach in our schools. In the classroom setting, we typically teach each academic subject as if it has an existence independent from others, failing to develop an awareness of integrativeness and interdependence. History can only be truly understood within the framework of the coexisting economic, social and psychological climate in which human action takes place. As Mihaly Csikszentmihalyi notes in *The Evolving Self: A Psychology of the Third Millennium*, we teach children conservation in physics—that each action produces an equal and opposite reaction—as if it were a law that applied only to pistons in an engine, while failing to develop an awareness that the same principle applies equally to human psychology, to social action, to economics, in fact, to the entire planetary system.

Our educational system is currently undergoing a major revamping as we try to restructure education to reflect this changing paradigm. Currently-held beliefs about how learning occurs fly in the face of our existing structure. Although the basic skills approach and the teaching of isolated subject matter has served us well in past generations, it will not prepare students for survival in the future or to take their place in a global society. In order to provide an optimal climate for learning in the 21st century, teachers are being called on to reframe their role and become concerned with the *facilitation* of learning rather than the *function* of learning.

We are faced with an entirely new situation in education where the goal of education is the promotion of change. Education can no longer enshrine the creative solutions of the past, rather it needs to make it possible for creativity to keep asserting itself by creating a mindfulness allowing individuals to perceive the universal network of interdependence in which our actions are imbedded.

Technological advances are occurring at such a rate and our scientific notions are in such a state of flux that a firm statement made today will almost certainly be modified by the time the student gets around to using the knowledge. Scientific beliefs age rapidly. They serve our needs for awhile, until we discover more compelling formulations, then the old beliefs act as brakes on progress.

The new science, embodied in "chaos theory," affirms that life in the universe is interdependent. Meaningful understanding comes about by fusing insights gathered from multiple representations of reality. As Margaret Wheatley has so aptly pointed out in *Leadership and the New Science*, revolutionary discoveries in quantum physics, chaos theory and evolutionary biology are reshaping our understanding of the universe, not as reactionary, but as orderly and self-governing. Living systems are open systems with the capacity to respond to change with renewed life. Fluctuations, disorder, chaos, change—all give birth to new, higher forms of order. Fritjof Capra in *The Turning Point* tells us that modern physics has abolished the notion of fundamentally separate objects. The new science views reality not as boundaries and separate things but as a network of inseparable patterns. In modern science the concept of observer has been replaced with the concept of participator. Quantum theory positions the universe as an interconnected web of relations whose parts are only defined through their connections to the whole. The new physics presents another version of reality as a union of opposites. Rest and motion, mass and energy, time and space—are so mutually interdependent they form an interwoven continuum, a single unified pattern.

Our psychological universe expands as does the physical universe—both are open systems, not predetermined. This concept of interconnectedness applies to all disciplines as well as to personal growth and development. Chaos in the physical world is mirrored in our individual worlds. Order emerges out of chaos.

We resist chaos in our lives, we resist emotional chaos, and we even resist chaos in our thinking. Because the experience of being out of control is so intolerable to most of us, we attempt to bring order to this chaos. Stephen Wolinsky in *The Tao of Chaos* suggests that we try to "freeze" chaos in order to manage it. If, however, we are willing to ride the rapids of chaos rather than resist it, a higher form of order emerges.

Challenging Formula Prescriptions

The path to self-fulfillment cannot be defined by prescribing a formula of the kind typically recommended by most self-help advocates. It takes viewing life in a much more holistic way, creating an awareness that life in the universe is interdependent. The traditional approach to self-analysis and self-help has taken a mechanistic, fragmented stance, isolating a particular behavior and applying a problem-solving approach. We reduce everything to its lowest common denominator by reducing complexity to bits and pieces. Complex issues are "solved" by reverting to a singular remedy characterized by prescriptions on how to get the love you want, how to solve relationship difficulties, how to deal with anger, how to resolve conflicts, how to assert yourself, and so on.

Formula solutions of this nature can be useful *if* they open the door to deeper meaning and serve as catalysts for further self-reflection. Behavior change strategies and planned interventions can be effective tools if they are viewed as means toward an end rather than as an end in themselves. They are only intermediary steps in the more soul-searching quest to attribute meaning to our existence and create inner and outer balance.

For example, if you are in a highly stressful situation it may take some stress-reducing strategies to get the stress at a manageable level so that an opening is created through which you can begin to look at how you are living your life. While the stress-reducing strategy has an immediate positive effect, if you rely only on strategies to reduce stress after it happens and fail to engage in further reflection to address the stress-producing situation, you may fail to examine your belief system and life choices that keep your stress level high. So it can be a "catch 22" in that you learn a strategy to get the stress under reasonable control, but the helpful strategy is actually self-defeating because the problem appears to be under control so you fail to attack what is producing the stress. This is the same kind of thinking that has driven our medical system until more recently and perpetuated a system that is not a health care system at all but rather a disease control system. We look only at symptoms and prescribe treatments based solely on the physical manifestations, neglecting the mind-body connection, the interdependence.

The journey toward personal fulfillment and true transformation requires major restructuring that can not be prescribed with an intervention formula. It can't be approached like we would plan a trip, by merely going to our local AAA office and requesting a "trip-tic" where someone else has mapped out the shortest, most direct route. When we try to approach personal growth with a trip-tic mentality, we may be able to change some specific behaviors but the change will be neither enduring nor transformative. Any meaningful change has to be guided by a sense of who we are and what our purpose is, and be part of a larger process that embodies an internal change in our life script. The pathway cannot be preplanned. Each of us has our own internal gauge for when we are ready to deal with a critical life issue. This is the phenomenon that keeps one in an abusive relationship or in addiction, or in a dead-end job. We are not able to move out of such obviously harmful patterns until we internally change our life script.

In the same vein, simplistic solutions advocated for problems in relationships in the form of specific behavioral interventions or simple strategies for negotiating and compromising to resolve conflict serve to trivialize complex issues and, hence, are doomed to be short-lived. If we move too quickly to negotiate a compromise to cope with a critical relationship conflict and that solution goes against a basic belief or value, it may serve to inhibit a true acceptance of essential differences requisite to living together in harmony.

Statistics attest to the lack of success behavioral and skills-based approaches to marital therapy have enjoyed. In fact, the statistics for the efficacy of much of modern couple therapy is disheartening—for 50% of the married couples who seek therapy, divorce is still the end result. This high failure rate can at least partially be attributed to a kind of tunnel vision some therapists have. In their attempts to apply a particular brand of therapy, they try to force every relationship to conform not only to a limited vision of how relationships ought to be to "work," but also to mold couples into taking on board their worldview and beliefs about "functional" human interactions.

Conventional wisdom undergirding marital relationship therapy is largely unsupported by empirical research. Much of current relationship therapy operates on the assumption that a couple's ability to express anger, face conflicts and solve problems of incompatibility are critical skills. Most relationship therapy tries to teach behavioral, psychological or social skills, the underlying assumption being that the person lacks the skills. But often it is not that the person lacks the skills, rather it is that the person is not able to apply the skills because of the mental anguish and physical stress brought on by being in a perpetual state of conflict. With the channels of communication completely broken down, one or both partners is constantly thinking negative thoughts about the other, rendering their minds and bodies in a state of defensive alert, causing a shutdown.

John Gottman characterizes much of what we currently see in couple therapy as "completely misguided" in its emphasis on skill development. He uses the example of attempting to teach husbands the skill of interpreting their wives' nonverbal behavior, citing evidence that husbands in unhappy marriages are terrible at reading their wives' nonverbal behavior but are great at reading others' nonverbal behavior. In essence, the problem isn't the lack of skills, rather it is the person's inability to use the skills because he is caught in a cycle of negativity that causes "flooding," characterized by sending one's blood pressure, heart rate, and adrenaline into a state of defensive red alert, prompted by feelings of hopelessness, isolation and loneliness.

When we approach personal growth issues as a series of individual problems to be solved, we fail to see the whole picture. As long as the issues are couched in technical terms, we are in the mode of solving problems and fixing situations, hence we seek the answers in the form of an intervention plan. We don't attack fundamental issues of judgment, control, trust, and forgiveness. In intimate relationships, we lose track of what really makes us happy—appreciation, humor, respect, affection. We stay on the surface; we don't touch our core, the center from which life's purpose reverberates.

When conflict is viewed in this mechanistic way, the solutions generated will be surface solutions that will typically serve only as a bandaid to patch up a wound, failing to address the underlying source. For example, a nonassertive, shy person may painfully learn more assertive behavior, characterized by stating her needs and intentions. While the introspection which may take place in learning to be more assertive can provide the impetus for more indepth self-reflection, merely learning the skills will not address the fundamental belief that leads people to fail to assert their wants and needs. These new skills will not work if the person doesn't confront principal beliefs about individual rights and worth. If we don't accept our personal rights we will not believe we have a right to stand up for ourselves or to take care of our emotional needs by expressing our feelings. In fact, we may actually believe that we are neither entitled to, or should have, certain feelings of hurt, anger or disappointment.

Often it is the fear of rejection or disapproval which serves as the basis for nonassertive or compliant behaviors. These fears include the fear of losing others' affection, the fear that others will think we are selfish, the fear that we will hurt others' feelings, or the fear that we will cause others to become angry. In our culture, females are socialized to help other people, put others' needs first, be sensitive to others' feelings and to be understanding and overlook minor disturbances. We try not to act superior, not to complain, and above all not to be a "bitch." If we believe that standing up for ourselves will result in disapproval, then we are likely to refrain from expressing our opinions or personal desires, hold back negative feelings, and avoid conflict even when others invade our personal bounds.

Sometimes individuals may actually allow their rights to be abused as part of a game they play. Then they feel justified in attacking the other person. After their aggressive outburst of feelings, they expect that person to feel guilty and become more affectionate. Thus, their aggression is a ploy to manipulate emotional closeness, rather than directly ask for affection or act in ways that openly show vulnerability to establish greater intimacy.

Just as nonassertive behavior often signifies a form of insecurity, so does the other extreme, aggressive behavior. There is an old Chinese proverb that "a show of strength suggests insecurity." Those who frequently act aggressively typically fear losing control and power over other people. The feeling of being vulnerable to an anticipated attack by another person often leads to aggressive behavior. The resulting aggressive reaction is instigated by threat and a sense of powerlessness. If we treat the symptom by merely trying to teach "anger control" or provide "aggression replacement training" we may help others function more successfully; however, real transformation only comes via the self-reflective process which enables them to come to grips with their insecurity, their fear of losing control, their vulnerability to others' behavior, or their sense of powerlessness.

We have to challenge basic beliefs about self-worthiness before we can truly endorse assertive behaviors. These new behaviors will not feel right until this deeper understanding is achieved. Bringing about these kind of significant attitudinal adjustments, or perceptual shifts, will take much more than a mere change in a particular behavior. In fact, continually trying to change isolated behaviors and individual relationships may actually act as an illusion which serves to further mask the kind of self-reflection required to truly examine perspectives that keep us from moving into balance.

To Change or Not to Change?

This question is really two-fold: Should we *try* to change our behavior? And if we try, Can we *really* change? The old paradigm was one of introspection and hard work. The commitment was to take control and change our destructive behaviors to more constructive behaviors. In the old paradigm, we had an action plan to live deliberately. In the new paradigm, there is no preplanned agenda. The new undertaking is to live life consciously and mindfully, creating a balance between our inner and outer worlds.

If we espouse this enlightened philosophy and we have some things about ourselves that we think still "need work," should we continue in our old vein of trying to change? Or, do we abandon the notion of a planned agenda of change? There will be some things about ourselves that we won't be able to change. However, there are most likely behaviors which each of us engage in which we would like to change, and from experience know that we can change by deliberate effort. If we merely give up the effort, will our new consciousness suffice as the vehicle for change?

My reconciling is that we strike a balance between a constant struggle and the flow of awareness. We stop pestering ourselves to change things that represent our internal order of doing things, like trying to become "more organized." Instead, we focus our energy on those things that keep us out of balance. On the one hand, we accept that our way of organizing may seem chaotic to others and may in fact cost us time when we need to find something quickly, and let go of the wishing to be more organized. On the other hand, we do put energy into changing the things that keep us from realizing who we are. We give ourselves permission to let go of the little struggles and enjoy ourselves.

The idea is to become a trusting, loving guardian to yourself, giving yourself unconditional acceptance. This unconditional acceptance doesn't involve just accepting your virtues, it involves accepting yourself in your entirety, including the characteristics you don't embrace. However, accepting the whole package doesn't mean you don't aspire to change, rather you accept what you have while in the process of change. You adopt the attitude that "I may not be there yet, but I'm moving." Instead of disliking yourself for behaving in ways you don't like, you affirm that it's hard to change, and take pleasure in your progress and accept your transgressions as part of the process.

The most terrifying thing is to accept oneself completely.
—CARL JUNG

∽

The process by which you achieve self-acceptance is not by conscious effort, and yet there is intentionality. It's the journey that brings you to a place within that's just where you want to be. It's a transformation that can't be achieved by willing; you can't force self-acceptance, rather it is something that happens to you. You simply become aware that a quiet has settled over you and you are ready to accept yourself just as you unfold. At some point you took on the frame of mind that you'll take what you've got and go with it. You give up the anxiety about changing, not the path. With this sense of contentment, you face the challenge to become all that you can. You live your life with a sense of the potentiality to unfold into a grander being. As Carl Jung noted, you learn to live as an individual in process, never a finished product.

There are definitely some behaviors which most would agree warrant change. The most obvious is when behavior is self-destructive, such as drug addiction. But there are many less severe behaviors that are ineffective, counterproductive and/or self-defeating. Change is in order when our current behavior pattern sustains our misery and a change in behavior would relieve our pain. Change to a preferable way of behaving is warranted when our present way of behaving is keeping us unfulfilled. Change may be necessary when our behavior is keeping us from getting what we really want. When we keep letting the same thing happen to us, we sometimes need to change our behavior to change the way others are responding to us.

The question of whether we should try to change our behavior is tied to cultural expectations. In our culture, angry or depressed behavior is unacceptable. We are continually bombarded by a media blitz that depicts a fun-loving, pleasure-seeking society. The collective societal mindset is that one is supposed to be happy, and that being depressed is somehow unAmerican! As Peter Kramer, the author of *Listening to Prozac* notes, our society has created a myth that certain behaviors are taboo, unacceptable. Hence, those who enact the forbidden behaviors evaluate their behavior against this expectation and conclude that they are emotionally disturbed and seek relief in the form of prescribed drugs. The drug offers them great relief from their pain and misery and stabilizes their behavior. However this false sense of control may keep the person from ever learning to accept his or her darker side. This drug-induced relief can be useful in transitioning from a serious emotional blow, but continued dependence can keep the person from discovering the source of his or her disturbance. (My reference here is not to the small percentage of individuals who have diagnosed psychological disorders and who may require longterm medication.)

A case in point is my friend Alice. She was distraught about her separation and pending divorce. Her doctor prescribed a drug to suppress her feeling of despair and helplessness. The divorce came and went and Alice got through it on an even keel. Several years later she's still caught up in her unfavorable attitude toward all men and her feelings of resentment. Being sedated during the difficult times may have kept her from ever facing her fear of loneliness and constructively addressing her anger which might have enabled her to *move on* rather than just *go on*.

Cultural myths perpetuate our ideas about what constitutes emotional stability, and conversely, emotional disturbance. One such myth is the myth of uniformity. Our society has created an image of expected or allowable behavior. This illusion of uniformity creates a sense of difference which leads individuals to make comparative judgments about their behavior. This societal expectation that "normal" emotional reactions lie within a narrow band serves to restrict the range of acceptable behavior, leading anyone who falls outside of the range to view him- or herself as abnormal.

Hence emotional disturbance is defined as behavior that is disturbing to others. Disturbing others, or acting out of the collective societal comfort zone, becomes the measure of emotional stability. There is no distinction between "disturbing" and "disturbed" behavior. This circular argument leads to the faulty diagnosis that "If I disturb others, I must be disturbed." Of course there are behaviors such as intentionally inflicting psychological or physical harm which most would label as disturbed behaviors, but there are also many other behaviors that society has condemned. Raising your voice in anger or punching a wall would be construed as being out of control and losing one's control is not condoned.

Summing Up

Again there is some reconciling in order. There are lots of things happening not only around the globe but in our own backyard that give us legitimate reason to feel depressed. Many of us choose to cope with the ills surrounding us by ignoring them, perhaps by becoming totally immersed in our work or in a relationship. Others become cynical and bitter, engaging in tirades about what's going on, but this sometimes serves only as their defense for not taking any action. And others take action by becoming globally aware and doing their small part to support what they believe. As the catch phrase goes, they "think globally and act locally." Others may choose to devote major time, energy and resources to making a difference.

In terms of relationships, the loss of a love can throw us into a tunnel of darkness until we are able to move through the pain. If we follow the popular philosophy of "choosing happiness" by denying or suppressing our pain before we have processed what has happened to us, this may keep us from allowing the natural healing cycle to run its course and the rebuilding process may be incomplete.

The point is that sometimes being unhappy, frustrated or angry is the appropriate response, indeed the necessary response to provoke us to take some action we need to take to align our actions with our convictions.

Some Theories of Change

Underlying the various approaches to therapy, healing and personal growth are theories of change. Basically, all approaches try to effect changes in a person's consciousness by expanding awareness. Ken Wilber in *No Boundary* used the framework of a "spectrum of consciousness."

In this framework, different schools of psychology and philosophies are not contradictory approaches to the individual, rather they are complementary approaches to different levels of the individual. He defined levels of consciousness relative to the boundaries used in defining "self" by distinguishing what is *within* the boundaries and what is *outside* of the boundaries.

If self is perceived as the mind or ego only, then the body is outside of its bounds. Psychoanalysis and most forms of conventional psychotherapy deal at this level where the aim is to heal the split between conscious and unconscious aspects of one's mind so that a person is more in touch with "all of his mind." If we apply a "skin boundary" then the environment is outside of its bounds. Humanistic psychology approaches deal at this level of the total organism, attempting to heal the split between ego itself and the body to reveal the total organism. Gestalt and Rogerian approaches fit here. If self extends beyond the individual, or is transpersonal, then the environment is not outside of its bounds. The therapies here are concerned with the "transpersonal self." Psychosynthesis and Jungian approaches would fall in this category.

At the end point of the continuum, self is one with the universe. Taoism and Zen Buddhism disciplines would fall into this category where the aim is to heal the split between the total organism and the environment to reveal an identity with the entire universe, or "unity consciousness." Gary Zukav in *The Seat of the Soul* espouses this doctrine when he says our personal anger "spills out of our private energy sphere and into the collective energy."

In this vein, personal growth can be thought of as a "rezoning"— acknowledgment and then enrichment of ever deeper and more encompassing levels of one's own self. In this scheme, the therapeutic process is one of enlarging and expanding of one's horizons, extending one's boundaries outwardly in perspective and inwardly in depth.

In the same vein, Alan Watts attempted to find a common ground for conceptualizing Eastern philosophical doctrines and Western psychotherapies. He posited that their main resemblance was twofold— their concern for bringing about consciousness, or changes in our ways of "feeling our own existence" and our relation to human society and the natural world. He saw the major difference to be one of audience.

Psychotherapists targeted the disturbed individual, while Eastern philosophies targeted all individuals.

Allen Wheelis in his classic book *How People Change* differentiated between change that occurs as a result of behavior therapy and "self-transcendence" back in the 70s. While conceding that we know it does work, he put forth the notion that shaping behavior by manipulation makes the person an object. Even if we design and provide for the experiences ourselves, we are nonetheless treating ourselves as object. And to some extent, we therefore become an object. If we shape our destiny from within then we become more of a creator. Wheelis defined self-transcendence as:

> "...a process of change that originates in one's heart and expands outward, always within the purview and direction of a knowing consciousness, begins with a vision of freedom, with an "I want to become...," with a sense of the potentiality to become what one is not. One gropes toward this vision in the dark, with no guide, no map, and no guarantee. Here one acts as subject, author, creator."

In the late 60s and 70s, Gestalt therapy enthusiasts were taking the position that change does not occur by coercive attempt to change, either by the individual or by another person. Rather, as Fagan and Sheperd put it in *Gestalt Therapy Now*, change takes place "when a person abandons what he would like to become and attempts to be what he is." We can't deliberately bring about changes in ourselves or in others. They made a clear distinction between self-actualizing and self-image actualizing, advocating that we shouldn't try to actualize a concept of what we should be like, rather we should actualize ourselves. This notion of "self-actualization" became the hallmark of what is often referred to as the human potential movement and began the heyday of the self-help "market."

Still another perspective on personal change is offered by Martin Seligman. He doesn't ask, 'Can we change?" or "Should we try to change?" or "How should we try to change?" For him, the "fact" is there are some things about ourselves that can be changed and some things that can't be changed and there is much evidence to help us sort the two. First we have to know what about ourselves will not yield to change and to learn to cope with what can't be changed. Knowing the difference between what we can change and what we have to learn to accept about ourselves arms us with a new understanding of who we are and where we are going. He provides us with the "complete guide to successful self-improvement" in his recent book *What You Can Change and What You Can't.*

PART II

Creating Your Personal Pathway

The Struggle Stage

Chapter 5

Learning to Live as Individuals in Process

The old paradigm was that we had to "do our work," meaning a longterm commitment to indepth introspection involving "working through" much pain. The challenge confronting us was to face our fears head on, to deal with our denial and to take control by taking action to live our lives deliberately. With the emerging paradigm comes a new challenge— to live life consciously and mindfully, to bring our inner and outer worlds into balance.

The new challenge is to engage in the practice of daily conscious living. Our actions arise from within; our actions are not reactions to our personal and global environment. Consciousness is the source of our capacity to change. Through consciousness we gain power and begin to open up to a greater range of choices. As we learn to become increasingly more and more aware and return to ourselves we move toward wholeness.

When we learn to return to ourselves, we begin to penetrate the meaning of our own experience. Instead of asking for advice or looking to others for answers, we learn to seek our own counsel by enlarging our awareness and expanding our consciousness. We become the watchful observer instead of the critical evaluator. We accept ourselves as we are. We don't try to prove ourselves. We affirm our right to choice and steadily give up our attachment to outcomes. We are not affected by the judgment of others, neither criticism nor praise. We pay attention with an open mind and become aware of what is happening. We acknowledge that there is a natural law of consequences.

Until we embark on the journey of inner discovery, we know only our outer layer, our public self, the self we present to the world. It is our reactive self, our self that acts out of fear. If we fail to penetrate our outer layer, we know only our defenses, our masks and our disguises of our true self.

It is as hard to see one's self as to look backwards
without turning around.

—THOREAU

∽

I'm endorsing a dual process of self-reflection and self-inquiry. Through self-inquiry I come to know myself and discover who I am. Through self-reflection I continually examine my actions and choices. Self-fulfillment is realized when I know who I am and my daily practice reflects my core beliefs.

Self-Reflection

I'm defining self-reflection as the ability to simultaneously look at what's happening without judgment while recognizing that the meaning that we attribute to it is only our interpretation filtered through our cumulative experience. When we are able to acknowledge this, then reality takes on a different meaning. When I can say "This is my experience and this is the meaning I attribute to what I am experiencing" I am aware that each person's reality is uniquely defined. Through self-reflection we can learn to see beyond the filters of our past and the blinders of our expectations. As John Heider, in *The Tao of Leadership*, expressed it "We learn to see things backwards, inside out and upside down."

Self-reflection encompasses reflection, contemplation, insight and understanding turned inward so we continually discover new dimensions of ourselves. When we experience discomfort, we go inside to become aware of what is happening. We don't judge ourselves or others and we don't look out there for a reason or a victim; we give up the pursuit to find who is at fault. We don't deny our feelings, instead we try to trace our feelings to a source, a beginning. "What is this feeling? Oh, yes. This is the same feeling I had when I was a child and I was afraid that I might provoke my parents' anger. Am I letting my fear of someone else's potential anger control my actions?"

Harville Hendrix alluded to a similar process in defining the "conscious marriage." He merged Freud's theory of the unconscious, proclaiming that our lives are directed largely by forces not in our consciousness nor under its control, with ancient mystical traditions perceiving our ordinary, everyday consciousness as an illusion referred to as a state of "waking sleep." While acknowledging important technical distinctions between the "unconscious" and "waking sleep," he noted that both viewpoints are in concert in perceiving that things are not the way they appear and that a fundamental change in "mental life" is necessary if we are to know the "truth." He referred to such changes as insight and awakening, respectively. Insight brings unconscious contents into consciousness, and awakening gives us direct experience of reality that has been hidden behind our symbolic constructions. His use of the term "becoming conscious" unites these two concepts as they apply to intimate relationships.

The reflective process which gives personal meaning to life involves deliberating many dilemmas, but probably the most basic is that of reconciling duty to self with responsibility to others. This quest is a soul-searching encounter striving to reconcile what is expected with what is right for each of us. Establishing this grounding helps to move into balance when our center has moved off course and we are wavering.

When I give of myself, I become more.

—LAO TZU

Self-Inquiry

The key to self-fulfillment is for our actions to reflect our core beliefs. Working to clarify your basic beliefs and continually checking whether your actions are congruent with what you believe requires ongoing examination to align your values with your life's work and daily living. By revisiting core beliefs you become aware of the choices you are making and recognize that other choices are available for the choosing.

When you use reflective inquiry you continue to ask "What in my life is working for me?" and, conversely, "What is not working?" "Am I moving in the right direction?" "Am I acting in ways that emanate from my core beliefs?"

Several years ago I realized that I had allowed my schedule to prohibit me from engaging in the kind of interpersonal dialogue I valued. It was important to me to have supportive relationships and be supportive in relationships and yet I hardly had any time to have a conversation, never mind actively listen and nurture others. My behavior was way out of line with my core values. My schedule of teaching, writing, research, and consulting had become so all-consuming that I had no time for what I defined as quality human interactions. I was espousing the value of intimacy and connectedness derived from caring human interactions, and yet, I had allowed competing agendas to take over and my schedule was out of control. In order to realign my actions with my beliefs I had to reexamine my priorities and confront the fact that my old drive to do it all had crept back into my life. My desire for status and recognition had pervaded my way of life and was overshadowing my need for intimacy and deeper connectedness.

Continual monitoring and revisiting of my core beliefs serves as the vehicle to get me back on track when I discover I am headed in the wrong direction. When I am off course, a signal for me is often the reoccurrence of a familiar dream. In the dream, my eyes are closed and I keep trying to open them, but they are "stuck." I'm saying to myself "I shouldn't be driving with my eyes shut." I've driven off a cliff and am falling into the ocean, but instead of being terrified that I am going to die I'm just experiencing a "floating" sensation. My interpretation of this dream is that I have lost sight of what's really important to me. This is a warning signal for me that I am out of sync with a core belief and that there is impending danger of losing myself again if I stay on this course.

We probably all have similar stories of getting a *wake-up call* that allows us to come to grips with the dissonance between a core belief and a current behavior. In my youngest sister's case, it took nothing short of a critical accident for her to reexamine the alignment of her current situation with her core beliefs. Her drive to move up the corporate ladder, have more material things and make the amount of money she thought she was *worth* had led her to 12-hour work days and a high anxiety state when she wasn't working.

Having a train accident was her wake-up call. After months of difficult physical therapy and several more months of trying to get back into her old schedule, she finally realized she had lost the vision of what was really important to her, having a family and time to spend with her husband. For her, the self-inquiry process of revisiting her core beliefs eventually led to a major life change. She gave up the executive position and went back to school to pursue the teaching career she had always wanted. She couldn't see her way to giving up what her position afforded her until she woke up to the dissonance between her behavior and what she really valued.

Often it does take a critical incident to shake us up so we can take a closer look. The moving into balance process of active self-inquiry can keep us from getting so far out of alignment that it requires an outside impetus for us to recognize that are actions are not in line with what we believe.

As professionals we construct a career path out of the options that avail themselves, hence professional careers often evolve through a combination of choice and circumstances in which some doors are opened as others are closed. Given that professional development is often only partly a function of desires and aspirations and is tempered by opportunity, or the lack of opportunity, it is not uncommon to find ourselves in a career track that is far from our intended path, and sometimes completely out of keeping with our core beliefs. Continually revisiting our core beliefs can strengthen the alignment between our values and our professional practice.

Constantly coming back to our core beliefs doesn't necessarily mean that we have to change our vocation, rather that we carry out our professional actions and interactions in a way that is consonant with our beliefs. However, sometimes the boundaries of our job demands and expectations may be so restrictive that there is no way to achieve greater alignment.

For me, coming back to my core beliefs about learning and self-change alters how I do what I do, not what I do. We basically have two choices, either to redefine what we do within the confines of our job responsibilities, or to do something that allows us to more explicitly "practice what we preach." We continually ask the question "How can I do what I do in such a way that it is more consistent with my core beliefs?"

Self-inquiry involves observing our patterns of behavior and examining our behavior in light of what we truly believe. Often reflection during, or simultaneously with, our actions is difficult because of the multiple demands we have to juggle in any given situation. For example, in the workplace attention to completing a task or meeting a deadline may distract from attention to quality of human interactions or relationships. Self-inquiry often requires a perspective of a meta-position, a looking back after the action has taken place.

The process of self-inquiry can be envisioned as flowing through several levels. Similar to a model developed by Shapiro and Reiff to examine the congruence between core beliefs and job performance, this model flows from the level of core beliefs to the level of specific actions. As shown in the diagram, this multi-level process has four levels: The philosophical level, the framework level, the interpretive level, and the decision-making level.

Philosophy of life is the backdrop for all other levels and activities. The philosophical level embodies core beliefs and includes values, religious beliefs, ways of knowing, life meanings, and ethics. A core belief is a belief about human nature or a belief about the way things are. The next level represents our way of providing an organizational framework for these basic beliefs and includes the theories we espouse, such as theories of human development and human behavior, theories of motivation and learning, theories of organizational development, and chaos theory. It is our framework for attaching meaning to what's happening. These underlying principles serve as the basis for how we organize what we have learned and experienced.

The next level is how we interpret these underlying principles into our general approach to daily practice. This is where we link our beliefs and theories into a way of being. Our daily practice is an overriding stance, a pervasive attitude for how we approach life and the situations we encounter. It's a frame of mind and is often an ideal way of behaving requiring constant revisiting to sustain. Out of our ideals for daily practice evolve our momentary actions. It is our way of making real our ideals and translating them into thoughts, behaviors and actions. This last level represents the translation into moment-by-moment decision-making.

The following diagram is offered to guide the process of self-inquiry to facilitate the discovery of misalignment between our actions and our beliefs.

A Model for Self-Inquiry

LEVEL 4
Decision Making
STRATEGIES / MOVES
Interventions, specific behaviors

LEVEL 3
Interpretive
DAILY PRACTICE
Patterns of arranging life, roles,
human interactions

LEVEL 2
Framework
UNDERLYING PRINCIPLES
Organizing framework for beliefs about
human development, human behavior,
motivation, etc.

LEVEL 1
Philosophical
CORE BELIEFS
Values, life meanings, ethics

The following example illustrates the four levels of the process for examining a core belief.

Core Belief

A belief about the way things are or a belief about human nature:
- Every person is doing the best that he or she can at any given moment.

Underlying Principle

Principles that organize our experiences and beliefs—our framework for interpreting our experiences:
- We are all wounded by our unmet needs in childhood and our life experiences. Our wounds lead us to act in protective, and sometimes hurtful, ways toward ourselves and others.

Daily Practice

Linking of beliefs with actions. In other words, if I hold this core belief and understand that behavior is often driven by childhood unmet needs, I will act in a way that reflects the belief and the underlying understanding:
- Accept what is
- Refrain from judging others

Strategies / Moves

If I accept the person's behavior without judgment then I will respond with compassion:
- Engage in active listening to come to understand others
- Choose my behavior knowing that others are not acting *against* me, but *for* themselves

The above example illustrates a positive belief, one leading us to act in compassionate and accepting ways toward others. But the model can also be applied to a negative belief, one typically leading us to act in unloving and judgmental ways toward others. An example of such a belief might be the belief that people should be strong. If I hold this belief, I may discover that I hold myself as well as others to my ideal of what it is to be strong. In daily practice, it could mean to me that I hide my true feelings, I try to control others for fear of letting others take control, I judge others as weak when their behaviors fall short of my expectations, or I condemn others for their actions and try to punish myself and others for failing to live up to my standards. In this case, where my belief is getting in the way of more productive and affirming actions, the process of change would involve challenging my belief and becoming aware of the influence the belief has on my actions.

PERSONAL EXERCISE

Examining Core Beliefs

This exercise can help you examine whether your actions are congruent with what you believe.

1. Write a positive belief you hold about human nature.

   Core Belief:

2. List the principle(s) that underlie this belief.
   What are the theories of human development or the theories about how the world works that frame this belief?

   Underlying Principle(s):

3. List specific ways of being and thinking that support this belief.

   Daily Practice:

4. List specific actions and behaviors that are consistent with this belief.

   Specific Strategies:

Questions for Self-reflection:

- In your daily life, how often are you acting in ways that are aligned with this core belief?
- What do you need to do to better align this belief with your moment-to-moment choices?

Our Screening Process

The meaning we attribute to our experiences is influenced by various factors that effectively screen out some responses while making others more probable. By examining our screens, we increase our awareness and keep from filtering out potential responses. As shown in the diagram, we can think of our screens as forming a successive series of interpretive filters. Each level of screen serves to eliminate some potential responses while allowing others to filter through. Our past experiences, beliefs, assumptions and expectations, feelings and mood, and our personal agendas and aspirations can either serve to limit or expand the repertoire of responses available to us in any situation.

Certain responses are eliminated by being screened through our past experiences. For example, the sight of a snake can conjure up a multitude of differing reactions on a continuum from absolute terror to curiosity to pleasure, based on what our experiences have been. Additional potential responses are ruled out on the basis of the beliefs we hold. Our beliefs can be self-affirming or self-defeating, rational or irrational. The assumptions that we make and the expectations that we have can make more responses unavailable to us. Our feelings, both those directly related to the immediate situation and those resulting from other experiences, also serve to screen out additional responses. And, finally, the agenda we set for ourselves and the aspirations we have act as still another filter.

Factors Mediating Response Choices

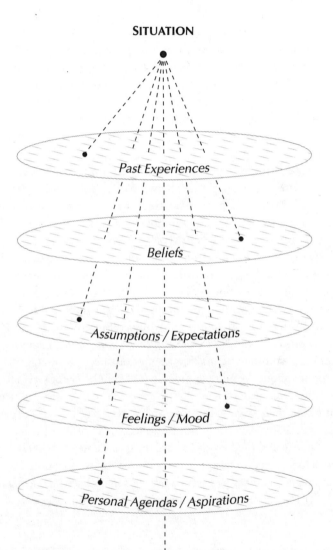

SITUATION

Past Experiences

Beliefs

Assumptions / Expectations

Feelings / Mood

Personal Agendas / Aspirations

RESPONSE

Our screening process results in differing perceptions of circumstances and events, leading to different interpretations, and subsequently to different responses. The way we respond is determined by our personal filtering system. This filtering system is a subjective mediating process. At the simplest level, there is an immediate reflexive response with no thought process occurring. A reflexive reaction, like removing your hand from a hot burner, is a reaction without conscious consideration of alternative responses. This type of response is often referred to as a "knee-jerk" response connoting that the response is automatic. Often we operate on "automatic pilot," closed off from entertaining a continuum of responses.

When we bring our personal screens into our awareness, we are expanding the mediating process between a situation and the resulting reaction. By bringing a greater portion of the mediating process into our awareness, we can increase our range of possible responses.

As an example, consider your typical response to criticism. Suppose your *reflexive reaction* is to automatically offer a defense to the criticism. Let's say you usually come in with a "but...," rather than merely 'taking in' the criticism, or exploring it further. Becoming aware of your own resistance and asking yourself questions like "Why do I need to be defensive?" or "What am I defending?" would represent challenging your screening process at the *assumptions and expectations* layer. Examining the assumptions you may be making about your need to be right or your assumptions about the person's judgment of your behavior serves to challenge your usual way of reacting, thereby allowing a greater range of responses to *filter through* your interpretive screen.

Our cumulative layers of screens can lead us to respond to situations in conditioned and rigid ways. To have the greatest freedom of choice and the capacity to respond uniquely to each situation we encounter, we need to examine our choices to see how our personal screens are influencing our ability to respond in unconditioned and unexamined ways.

Choosing the most appropriate response requires an opening of the mind and the heart. When we are able to create this opening, no possible response is automatically ruled out or in. As we begin to take time to consider alternate responses to reoccurring situations in our lives we become open to more possibilities, and can move away from our knee-jerk, or *unexamined,* reactions.

Summing Up

The self-inquiry process raises our level of consciousness and this increased awareness provides an opportunity for us to spot incongruence or imbalance. Continually revisiting our core beliefs and examining and testing our actions against these beliefs is the gateway to balance and harmony in our lives.

Through engaging in self-reflection we come to see our actions without the screens of our expectations and personal agendas. Through the practice of self-inquiry we return to our core beliefs and evaluate our choices in accordance with these beliefs.

The process of merging self-reflection and self-inquiry is not specifically prescriptive in nature, rather it is a process that allows insights to surface which serve to challenge our familiar behavior patterns. It is more a way of knowing than a knowing how. This process provides direction and materializes as our inner guide to knowing. Change is an emergent process of learning to become increasingly more aware and that consciousness is the source of our capacity to unfold and expand, opening up to all possibilities.

Man's main task in life is to give birth to himself

—ERICH FROMM

Chapter 6

Challenging Beliefs

In order to change we have to challenge our basic belief system. If we merely try to change a behavior without attacking the belief that drives the behavior, the change is not likely to be very long-lasting. Because our beliefs are learned, they can also be relearned through challenging our beliefs. Albert Ellis, a pioneer of self-analysis and a forefather of the self-help movement, noted that many of our basic beliefs we learned in childhood are actually irrational beliefs. Irrational beliefs have no factual basis, are illogical, and are harmful to those holding them.

As a child grows, the child begins to incorporate a sublanguage which serves to attribute meaning to the events occurring in the child's life. This sublanguage eventually becomes the child's belief system which develops as does language, primarily through modeling. The belief system of the significant person(s) in the child's life will largely determine whether the child thinks rationally or irrationally about the events in his or her life. If, for example, the child misbehaves and the parent(s) says "You know better than to do that!" the child will most likely come to believe "It's bad to make a mistake, I am bad because I make mistakes and because I'm bad I should be punished." The more rational belief is that mistakes are a normal part of learning and that making a mistake doesn't make me bad. If I didn't learn this as a child, I am likely to continue to interpret my mistakes as intolerable unless I am able to restructure my belief. If I hold onto this belief, I will most likely set unrealistic expectations for myself and others.

These irrational beliefs typically continue to plague us throughout our adult lives. One of the most common irrational beliefs that we hold is that people who harm us or commit misdeeds rate as bad individuals and we should blame and punish them. People not only turn this severely critical thinking on others but also turn it on themselves by damning themselves for being such bad persons. A more rational alternative is that we can tell people directly what they are doing that has negative consequences for us, but we don't have to berate them or go as far as to try to punish them.

Much of our behavior is influenced by the way we feel and our feelings are a product of our beliefs. When we hold an irrational belief, we are likely to behave inappropriately because the irrational thinking produces a negative emotional state (e.g., anger, anxiety). An event triggers a counterproductive belief, often at an unconscious level, and strong emotions surface, generally manifesting in an inappropriate behavior. Hence, our thoughts, feelings and behaviors are not separate entities, they are interrelated, interactional and codependent. Because our actions are a manifestation of the feelings produced by what we think, the way to change a self-defeating behavior is to modify the irrational thinking that led to the behavior.

People basically espouse either of two models of causation of emotions: "It upsets me" or "I upset myself." In the "It upsets me" view, an event or circumstance necessarily leads us to experience a certain emotion. In other words, if someone rejects us, we must feel sad and worthless—the situation determines our emotions. People who have this worldview characteristically blame other people and external factors for their upsets and their coping strategies are all outwardly directed. They may try to cope either by escaping the situation or by attacking the person or situation that they view as being the cause of their upset.

If, on the other hand, we believe that "I upset myself," we recognize the controlling role of our interpretation and appraisal of an event. Accepting this notion leads us to take responsibility for our emotions. Many people find it hard to accept that they are the creators of their upset feelings. Acknowledging that the same set of circumstances or event will cause a different response in different people supports this notion that it is our human appraisal and accompanying self-talk that creates our emotional response. Furthermore, as we look at our life experiences, we can see that our reactions to situations change over time. Perhaps we used to get upset and defensive when we were criticized, but now it doesn't bother us. Because we have changed our appraisal of what it is to be criticized and our inner dialogue when we are criticized, we simply don't upset ourselves about criticism from others anymore.

The irrational ideas we acquired in our early lives still continue largely because we keep reindoctrinating ourselves with these ideas and consciously and unconsciously work to perpetuate them. Most conditioning is self-conditioning. Acknowledging this self-creation and continued reinforcement is critical in the process of working to change our ideas. For example, we have a choice whether to hold onto the belief that our parents were the source of all our troubles and still are, or alternatively, to acknowledge that our parents kept criticizing us during childhood and we still keep taking them too seriously and thereby continually keep upsetting ourselves. Choosing the latter interpretation allows me to acknowledge that *I* still think poorly of myself when they criticize me and consequently feel worthless. When I am able to acknowledge my self-reinforcement I can begin to move away from my sense of helplessness, thereby enabling myself to move from blaming my parents for something they did to me to cause my current behavior, to taking responsibility and can begin to look within for change. Applying this kind of *cognitive mediation* allows us to restructure our thinking about our parents' behavior so that we are able to acknowledge that the problem was how we interpreted the behavior and what we did to ourselves that caused and continues to cause a problem.

Self-Talk

People tell themselves various sane and insane things. Beliefs and attitudes materialize in the form of internalized self-talk. This is the realm of conscious interpretation. We continually talk to ourselves throughout the day. Step back and listen for a few seconds and you will notice a kind of internal, running commentary. We talk to ourselves as we're driving, we talk to ourselves as we're doing the dishes, and we talk to ourselves about our memories and plans for the future. By means of this self-talk, we constantly evaluate our sensations.

The vast majority of our self-talk is learned. It is learned from our family, our friends, and from society. Guiding assumptions about the nature of self-talk can be cast into two belief statements: (1) Only I can upset myself and I do that with my self-talk, and (2) My self-talk is learned and I can learn to use different self-talk. Our old patterns of responding create a groove in our mind, making it difficult to take a different route. The pathway to change consists of clearly seeing, understanding, disputing, altering and acting against these familiar internal verbalizations.

Replacing dysfunctional thoughts with more functional ones involves developing an awareness of those events and thoughts associated with negative feelings and resulting inappropriate behaviors. We first need to be in touch with our feelings, then reflect on the event or action which led to the feeling, before we can identify the thinking that mediated between the event and the feeling. For some, this awareness will need to be developed prior to making the connection. Once we recognize our thinking patterns, the process of mental appraisal takes our automatic responses and brings them to awareness. By paying attention to our internal dialogue we identify our self-defeating thoughts.

One especially dysfunctional pattern of self-talk leading to anxiety-producing thoughts typically takes the form of making unrealistic demands. These demands can be made upon others, on ourselves, or of life in general. When we make unrealistic demands, we frequently couch these demands in self-talk characterized by the words *should, must, and have to.*Phrasing our expectations in these terms creates rigid demands and when these demands are not met, we experience upset. We expect family members, coworkers, neighbors, leaders, lovers and so on to behave in certain ways. If we frame our expectations of others in terms of rigid demands, then we tell ourselves, for example, that our colleagues *have to* respect us, our boss *must* treat us fairly, or our lover *should* understand us. When our demands are not met, we feel frustrated, hurt and angry.

Our desires and ensuing attachments, embodied in the language of *shoulds, musts, and have -tos* are at the root of emotional imbalance. By tempering our inner language to a language of preference rather than demand, we can weaken the attachment and begin to separate ourselves from our desire. The reality is, people behave the way they want to and not necessarily the way we want them to.

We also apply these rigid demands to our self-expectations by telling ourselves we *must* succeed or we *shouldn't* make mistakes. Again, if we can recast our self-expectations as preferences, we can become more self-accepting when we don't fulfill our own expectations. Likewise, when we make demands for how the world should treat us, we believe that bad things shouldn't happen to us. There's no guarantee that any of us will be spared life's trials. Opening up and accepting the possibility that these things can happen to us allows us to glean whatever value might come from life's difficulties and to more fully embrace life.

Irrational Beliefs

Irrational beliefs serve an important function for individuals espousing them. Although these beliefs lead to great discomfort and much unnecessary misery, they are the best the individual has had available. Developing more rational alternative beliefs is an ongoing process of persistent working to challenge these beliefs. This self-analysis process involves learning how to observe your own feelings and actions, and subsequently learning how to evaluate them objectively rather than moralistically. We rarely eliminate our irrational ideas entirely, more often the process of challenging them is continual.

Ellis maintains that merely resolving to correct your wrongs the next time will not suffice anymore than resolving to make yourself a good pianist. You have to literally force yourself to follow a new path, otherwise you continue in the same saga. Change will only come about by work and practice, by identifying, challenging and replacing the irrational beliefs that sustain your current ineffective behavior.

In *A New Guide to Rational Living*, Ellis identifies three basic irrational beliefs we learned in childhood that typically plague us and cause us to function ineffectively throughout our lives. These beliefs are related to how we perceive personal rejection, personal competence, and fairness. These beliefs are: (1) You *must* have love and approval *all* of the time from *all* of the people you consider significant, (2) you must prove yourself thoroughly competent, adequate, and achieving, and (3) you must view life as awful or catastrophic when things do not go the way you would like them to go. There are also several other second-order irrational beliefs which typically piggyback after one of the three basic beliefs is operating.

A more rational alternative for the first belief is that I can determine what I want to do rather than adapt or react to what I think others want. For the second belief, a more rational alternative is that if I demand that I be perfect, I will always be pushing or worrying when I'll slip; instead, if I do what I want and what I enjoy as well as I can, I'll be happier and perform better. A more rational alternative for the last belief is that when a person has treated me badly and I don't like the situation or that person's behavior, I can recognize that I can't change either, and begin to make plans for making my situation as desirable as I can.

Our emotions can either mobilize or immobilize us. Our irrational thinking spurs inappropriate negative emotions, inappropriate either because they lead to experiencing a great deal of pain and discomfort, or because they lead to engaging in self-defeating behavior. The contrasting more appropriate negative emotions alert us that our goals are being blocked, but they do not immobilize us. They motivate us to engage in self-enhancing behavior by mobilizing us to action. Below are some examples of emotions discussed by Dryden and DiGiuseppe that tend to immobilize us and their corresponding more constructive counterparts.

Situation	Irrational Emotion	Rational Emotion
Faced with threat or danger	Anxiety	Concern
Faced with loss or failure	Depression	Sadness
Breaking of own moral code	Guilt	Remorse
Other betrays self	Hurt	Disappointment

Roush described six common classes of irrational thinking: 1) Robot thinking ("It's not my fault."), 2) I Stink! thinking ("It's all my fault."), 3) You Stink! thinking ("It's all your fault."), 4) Fairy Tale thinking ("That's not fair!"), 5) Namby Pamby thinking ("I can't stand it!"), and 6) Doomsday thinking ("Woe is me!"). Fairy Tale thinking of the vintage of "Oh what a wonderful place this would be if only..." keeps one in a fantasy land where "everyone lives happily ever after." You Stink! thinking, is the kind of thinking that keeps one in a defense mode—always on guard to ward of impending attacks by others.

Robot thinking leads to the faulty logic that if it's not my fault, then I don't have to look at my own actions or accept any responsibility. Author/poet Portia Nelson in portraying her journey through emotional and psychological healing in *There's a Hole in My Sidewalk* points out the pitfalls of this kind of thinking in her poem "Autobiography in Five Short Chapters."

Chapter I

I walk down the street.
There is a deep hole in the sidewalk.
I fall in.
I am lost... I am helpless.
It isn't my fault.
It takes forever to find a way out.

Chapter II

I walk down the same street.
There is a deep hole in the sidewalk.
I *pretend* I don't see it.
I fall in again.
I can't believe I am in this same place.
But it isn't my fault.
It still takes a long time to get out.

Chapter III

I walk down the same street.
There is a deep hole in the sidewalk.
I see it is there.
I still fall in... it's a habit... but,
my eyes are open.
I know where I am.
It is *my* fault.
I get out immediately.

Chapter IV

I walk down the same street.
There is a deep hole in the sidewalk.
I walk around it.

Chapter V

I walk down another street.

My exposure to the concept of disputing irrational beliefs came after I had traveled a long way down my path of personal growth, making this idea meaningful to me "at face value." By that I mean I was able to integrate the concept without "living the process." The concept provided a hook for me to pull together some of my insights about the power of belief systems. So while I may endorse the theory as an organizational scheme that helps me understand human behavior, I don't necessarily endorse the prescribed intervention procedures for "cognitive restructuring" advocated in Ellis' Rational Emotive Therapy (RET). Perhaps the reason for my connecting with the concept of irrational beliefs for explaining ineffective behavior is because the concept of nonjudgment is imbedded, in terms of judging oneself, judging others, and evaluating situations according to unrealistic expectations.

In examining these self-defeating beliefs in my own life, I discovered that some I didn't hold and perhaps never did (Life should be fair; Life is awful when things don't go my way), some I had let go of somewhere along my personal growth journey (e.g., I don't need to punish others for their misdeeds), some I had never thought about (e.g., I need approval from everyone, all of the time), and some seemed to creep surreptitiously into my thoughts (e.g., I have to prove myself to be competent), but I seemed already to know they were irrational beliefs. Having this conceptual framework now helps me to more readily dispute my irrational thinking. A recent example for me was receiving a letter canceling a workshop I was planning to do on a remote island. I had prepared the final copy for the catalogue, had a professional photograph taken, and had planned my summer around the dates. The letter merely informed me that they were not able to "fit it in." The irrational belief I had to dispute here was *I have to prove myself to be competent.* I was judging myself as incompetent because someone had decided not to include the workshop. In the process I moved through anger, hurt, embarrassment, and disappointment, to surrender, and then to self-acceptance.

So what happens is that I catch myself with an "ahah this is one of those culprits." For me, the awareness helps me to squelch the self-defeating thoughts. But what if I actually held onto one of these beliefs and had let it govern my actions for all of my life, would I be able to restructure my cognitive awareness? And, what would it take? I would offer that there are many pathways to accomplishing this result and that the cognitive intervention involving the structured process of identifying faulty thinking patterns is only one of the alternate routes.

As I began to view others' behavior patterns within this framework, I became aware that when one held onto one of these core beliefs, the harmful effect was pervasive. Armed with this insight into others' thought processes, I clearly saw the havoc that the belief could wreak in a person's life. I became aware that an associate was caught up in the irrational belief that "People who harm you or commit misdeeds rate as bad, wicked individuals and you should severely blame, damn and punish them for their sins." I began to see that her life was governed by a very pervasive belief and she seemed not to have a way of disputing it. Her conversation was dominated by statements about what she deserved and, conversely, what others didn't deserve. (I guess these go hand in hand!) When others behaved in a way she thought was wrong, she believed they should be punished and, in fact whenever possible, set about to punish them or see that they got what they deserved. This person is prone to moodiness and depression. Her attention, her thoughts are taken up with trying to get back at others and trying to force others to act according to her belief system.

Another friend holds the irrational belief that "Things should turn out better than they do and that you have to view it as awful if you do not quickly find good solutions to life's hassles." Those who hold onto this belief frequently speak bitterly about others and tend to generalize to classes of people (e.g., women, bosses, cops). They feel and act victimized. My friend's dialogue is filled with "it shouldn't have happened," "it wouldn't have happened if…," and "these things always happen to me." He truly believes the saying, "If it weren't for bad luck, I'd have no luck at all." This belief does seem to serve as a self-fulfilling prophecy. Holding on to this belief keeps him in a general state of negativity.

We probably all know someone who lives by the irrational belief that "Life is awful when things don't go the way you want them to go." Those who act on the basis of this irrational belief are characterized by profuse complaining or bemoaning of their "tragedy." They take things to their worst possible outcome, or "awfulize" every trying situation. This kind of "Why me?" thinking keeps them in a holding pattern, waiting for the next awful thing to happen, keeping them from being able to experience the joy of what is happening now.

Internalizing the belief that "Life should be fair" perpetuates a feeling of powerlessness, leading one to act helpless and/or angry much of the time. Believing that life should be fair sets up expectations that can't be met, and hence can keep a person in a constant state of disillusionment. I also see this belief as yet another form of judgment. If I believe I can set the standard for fairness, there is also an implied assumption that life's rewards should be distributed proportionately with my idea of worthiness.

Breaking out of the mental trap of these beliefs will clearly have a far-reaching impact on a person's quality of life. However, we can't prescribe a formula for unlocking the door; the way out will require a perceptual shift, and there is no blueprint.

Summing Up

The notion that it is our repetitive thoughts that make us crazy dates back to the '60s and is at the root of many more current ideas. Many popular themes represent various renditions of the concept that our behavior is governed by emotional states brought on by our conscious and unconscious assumptions, evaluations and interpretations of situations. This is the basic principle behind many of the popular doctrines like the power of positive thinking, the self-talk solution, you are what you think, you'll see it when you believe it, self-acceptance and self-forgiveness, self-affirmation, and happiness is a choice.

More recent theories of human behavior attribute our mental anguish not to a "deep, dark unconscious mind" as described by Freud and Jung, but to a more accessible region of the mind, lingering just short of full consciousness. It can be thought of as the mind we see out of the corner of our eye and is where we store our experiences. It is the source of emotion and is formed solely by our experiences, learning from what happened early in our lives. We continue to interpret the world in terms of these early experiences, forming what Epstein called "stubborn suppositions which act as a subliminal broadcaster of automatic thoughts." So, for example, if you have been abused by your father, you may come to associate all men with abuse. Or, if you were left by your father, you may come to associate all men with abandonment. These automatic thoughts are the root of sexism and racism, producing conditioned reactions to situations based on our experiences that color all our conscious thoughts.

Continuing with this line of thinking, the route to personal growth and understanding doesn't have to require extensive psychotherapy to uproot the unconscious, rather it is possible to accomplish considerable change in our way of behaving through rational reflection, or learning to listen in on the internal dialogue in the mind. Our choice is to either remain trapped behaving automatically or to break out of our destructive mental patterns and begin to reprogram our thinking. If we can reprogram our thinking, we can change our emotions because they are intimately entangled.

Internalized stories and the assumptions they embody are the driving force behind much of our behavior. Our mind is a realm of metaphors, myths, and movies. Everyone is fond of a good story; if you want to hold a person's attention, tell them a story. While our stories may have nothing to do with current reality, we think and act as if they do.

The repetitive stories we tell ourselves about how the world works serve to perpetuate our automatic ways of interpreting the world. Although these stories are our own invention, fabricated in our minds, they serve the function of putting our immediate experiences into our past experience framework. We weave our own tall tales, but we don't distinguish our tales from reality. These stories in the background of our mind keep us locked in our judgments, assumptions and interpretations. Our self-created storylines wreak havoc in relationships by creating a mental picture of how things ought to be—stories such as "If someone loves you, he/she should always make you happy." or "If someone loves you, he/she should know how to make you happy." These fairy-tale stories provide the backdrop for the expectations we have for our relationships, setting us up for disappointment.

Peter Senge in *The Fifth Discipline* refers to our deeply ingrained assumptions, generalizations, and images as "mental models" that sway how we understand the world and consequently act. We frequently are not aware either of our mental models or their effect on our actions. What we say or espouse is often out of line with our mental models. While what we say may be incongruent with what we do, we do act congruently with what we believe, our mental models.

There is much evidence to support the notion that we have to keep attacking and challenging the repetitive thoughts that endlessly parade through our minds in order to surrender automatic or conditioned ways of interpreting our world and begin to open up to new realms of possibility.

Chapter 7

Reconciling and Moving into Balance

The Multiple Meanings of Reconciling

Reconciling has multiple meanings. Reconciling can mean to cause to cease hostility or opposition, to become resigned to something not desired, to harmonize, or to settle inconsistency. All of these meanings come into play in my use of the term reconciling.

Reconciling involves a ceasing of the opposition, an acceptance of polarities. Part of the reconciling process is achieving a personal balance between polarities. Sometimes this is a conscious choosing of one way of behaving over another. Sometimes it is a letting be, reconciling the coexistence of opposites, recognizing that there can be no bringing together. Sometimes it is the acceptance of a present state of being while simultaneously knowing that we are aspiring to be in another state.

We reconcile where we are while we are in the emergent process of change. While we hold a vision of where we would like to be, we don't pass judgment on ourselves for not being there yet. We trust that wherever we are is where we need to be and that we are moving forward in the right direction. Rather than judge ourselves as inadequate because we are in an emergent state, we accept the uncertainty and see it as an opportunity to learn and integrate new ideas.

Perspectives on the Self-Change Process

Current authors writing in the category of psychology, self-help, and inspiration run the gamut in terms of espoused theories of self-change. Either implicitly or explicitly, they take varying positions about self-improvement that range from work, work, work, to developing an awareness, to being present, to experiencing the rawness of conflict, to letting be, to effortless being.

Probably the most extreme position is exemplified in John Heider's *The Tao of Leadership*, a translation of Lao Tzu's *Tao Te Ching*, "adapted for a new age." He tells us to forget those clever techniques and self-improvement programs and quit trying to solve our problems by trying to change. No techniques can enforce positive qualities. His advice for improving yourself is to "try silence or some other cleansing discipline that will gradually show you your true selfless self."

Writing about intimate relationships in *Soulmates*, Thomas Moore takes a similar stance against traditional approaches to personal growth, disparaging our attempts to analyze relationships as mere rationalizations and simplifications, not true understandings. He maintains that endless analysis and introspection serve to "dry out a relationship." The heart is not a puzzle to be figured out; it is a mystery, beyond manipulation. Everything associated with the heart—relationships, emotions, passion—can be grasped only with the "tools of religion and poetry." We shouldn't concern ourselves with how to make relationships work, rather we should accept the relationship as the "place where the soul works out it's destiny." We don't ask how to improve a relationship, rather we wonder what the soul is wanting.

John Welwood, in *Journey of the Heart*, takes a similar position that self-help techniques rarely have any real impact. When they are used as quick-fixes, they bypass "letting a difficulty affect us, work on us, and move us to find our own genuine response to it." One has to develop an inner awareness and willingness to change before self-help prescriptions can be utilized effectively. Mere symptom relief is not enough because "a relationship is always a living *process*, never a finished *product*."

In contrast, the pathway to change advocated by many other popular authors represents change as a hefty task requiring deliberate effort to change specific behaviors. Two best-selling authors, Harville Hendrix

(*Getting the Love you Want*) and Joan Borysenko (*Minding the Body, Mending the Mind*), describe a behavioral change process that represents the paradigm of hard work. They offer specific behavior change prescriptions. Hendrix advocates for a process that combines insight and behavioral change, maintaining that it's not enough to understand the unconscious motivations of marriage, nor is it sufficient to introduce behavioral changes into a relationship. Insight alone will not heal the childhood wounds that we bring to marriage. Moreover, without understanding the reasons behind the behaviors, couples will have only limited growth. Combining learning more about unconscious motivations with a process for transforming these insights into supportive behaviors, he consequently recommends a ten-step process and prescribes specific exercises to assist in translating the insights into effective skills. The view represented here is a behavioral approach in which the underlying theory serves as the motivation and the growth process involves learning specific skills. In other words, growth is achieved by mastering skills.

Borysenko sanctions an approach requiring motivation, effort and determination, clearly in support of the hard work ethic. She maintains that learning anything requires practice; to get the tools of the trade to live a healthier life, you must practice. She advocates a two-step process involving inviting awareness, " a mental stretching that limbers up your perceptions," and working to change a mindset that is conditioned to fear and doubt.

While she places greater emphasis on awareness and less on specific behavioral interventions, nonetheless she recommends specific methods and strategies to facilitate the growth process. Her premise is that trying to change ingrained, self-defeating ways of thinking and behaving is a tedious process of confronting our fears directly and seeing them for what they are.

Concerning relationships, Hendrix, Moore, and Welwood all take a similar position in their view about contemporary relationships. That position is that the difficulty, pain and conflict experienced in a relationship can serve as a pathway to new levels of understanding and deepen our connection with ourselves and expand our sense of who we are. All espouse that the intimate love relationship can be a critical force in reaching our human potential. Yet their notions about why this is and how we learn and grow in relationships is markedly different. Each envisions the process quite differently. For Hendrix, it is the healing of childhood wounds accompanied by specific behavioral changes in which we learn more supportive behaviors. For Welwood, it is dancing on the razor's edge, fully experiencing the rawness of conflict. And for Moore, it is being in tune with the direction our soul wants to take.

My Reconciling

My position is somewhere in the middle. For me it relates back to the idea of change as a process that moves us along the growth continuum. It's possible to move either from a heightened awareness that may lead to a choice to change a behavior, or from a change in behavior which can influence how we validate our perceived effectiveness and lead to a greater consciousness. However, as long as I am doing what I think I *should* do rather than what I have come to know is right for me, a behavior change will be hard to sustain. So while enduring change emerges from an inner sense of what is right, individuals do sometimes benefit from being given a specific strategy; however, a given prescription is only a beginning, a first step toward self-discovery.

I purposefully resist the temptation to tell others what they should do because my belief is that people change through a personal discovery process, an emerging from within. I prefer gentle suggestions that individuals can try to see if the fit is right. The following suggestions are examples.

- Pay attention to what your inner voice is saying.
- Trust your own counsel.
- Reposition the situation, see it from a different perspective.
- Envision other possible actions.
- Be aware of your feeling and give it a name.

Thinking along these lines serves as a reminder to push beyond your blinders and let down your disguises so that you keep looking at who you are and keep making choices about your actions.

Can Awareness Suffice as the Vehicle for Change?

Representing the belief that one cannot force a behavior change, Susan Page author of *If I'm so Wonderful, Why am I Still Single?* maintains that if you simply try to order yourself to change you will be working against yourself rather than with yourself. Programming yourself to change, or ordering yourself to make a change, is almost always doomed to failure. When you merely order yourself to change you don't engage in a process that allows you to discover why you were using this self-defeating behavior in the first place. She relates the story of getting feedback that she was smiling profusely and inappropriately and that made others uncomfortable. When she deliberately tried to stop smiling it felt unnatural and so she decided to keep smiling. Then she was encouraged by a Gestalt therapist to not try to change her behavior, rather to start paying attention to it. Over time, the smiling behavior came to feel unnatural and the smiling changed by itself without conscious effort. Her analysis was that she had believed that people would ignore her unless she smiled at them all the time. By experimenting with not smiling, she discovered she was afraid that people wouldn't like her, not even notice her. She came to the realization that she was compulsively manipulating everyone she met to pay attention to her. It was only after she experienced that she could function quite adequately without perpetual forced smiling that she was able to give it up. So what happened was that the more comfortable behavior of not smiling all the time emerged as she logged data showing her that her belief was not true.

We often get trapped by our own belief system which perpetuates itself by its own internal logic. Behavior changes only as belief changes.

My Reconciling

Although Page never mentioned disputing irrational beliefs, she described a process that served to challenge her faulty logic—that you have to smile to be recognized. The process of challenging irrational beliefs by overt "cognitive restructuring" clearly represents the school of thought that sanctions the notion that personal change is realized only through deliberate work, exercising discipline and conscious control. This is clearly in contrast to the perspective that behavior change cannot be forced. However, I see actively disputing irrational beliefs not as a direct intervention in the sense of a specific prescription, but rather as a reflective process of personal examination. This reflective process traces present self-defeating behavior to an old memory circuit which made a faulty connection between an action and the interpretation of the action as self-defeating rather than self-affirming.

While Page advocates a *natural* process, Ellis and his colleagues advocate a *deliberate* process. He sees change as tedious, she as an unconscious emerging awareness. What is common to both convictions is the notion that it is the meaning we attach to the behavior, our interpretation, that governs how we perceive it.

Again, searching for the middle ground, I see the middle ground as the self-reflective process. Although not through a deliberate process of disputing irrational beliefs, the belief driving her continuous smiling was dispelled. Upon introspection, she was able to figure out what was happening and discover the belief that sustained her inappropriate behavior. This is in contrast to the active practice of overtly attempting to challenge an irrational belief through the process of coming to recognize self-defeating thinking styles by making our internal dialogue explicit and furnishing logical arguments that dispute the irrational thinking and replace it with more rational thinking. I see both of these processes as representations of reflective practice. In the former case, merely paying attention, it is reflective inquiry *on* practice, or reflection in retrospect; in the latter case, actively disputing an irrational belief, it is reflective inquiry *in* practice, or reflection while engaging in the behavior.

Perhaps because the behavior of smiling is more of a surface behavior, the process of challenging the thinking that mediated the behavior could be accomplished by merely paying attention to it. If, on the other hand, I am holding onto a more pervasive irrational belief such as "Life should be fair," I would argue that the process would take more "work."

As I contemplated the difference between the deliberate and conscious act of trying to change a behavior versus a mere paying attention to it or just noticing it, I began to think that the difference is actually quite subtle, and perhaps indistinguishable. If I make myself aware of something by paying attention to that something that had been occurring unconsciously or automatically, can I really do this without a conscious effort?

Another factor is that I have to be capable of looking at my behavior and pushing beyond my disguises to see what is really happening. This relates to the continuum of change notion presented earlier. I would maintain that I have to have moved to a place where I'm able to watch my behavior without judgment, to be the watchful observer rather than the critical evaluator. Until I am able to do this, the challenging of beliefs will require a deliberate process, a structured intervention.

Cognitive restructuring is a strategy for changing irrational beliefs which lead to ineffective or self-defeating behavior, to more rational beliefs which sustain more effective and self-affirming behavior. You can utilize this strategy as a self-help strategy by going through a series of self-questions. To begin to discover what types of self-talk are creating and maintaining your emotional response notice what you are saying to yourself by asking questions like the following.

- Am I making rigid and inflexible demands of myself? of others? of life?
- What *shoulds* am I telling myself?
- Am I accepting what has happened?
- Am I trying to understand some of the possible causes for the situation?
- Am I telling myself that what happened is interesting or am I engaging in awfulizing about it?
- Am I engaging in *always-never* thinking?
- Am I projecting that this awful state will go on forever?
- Am I believing that I, another person, or the situation itself can never change?
- Am I engaging in *all-or-nothing* thinking?
- Am I describing myself or others as without value, totally unworthy of love, respect or affection?

Challenging Irrational Thinking

As a way of challenging your irrational thinking, try moving through the following steps to talk yourself through a situation.

1. Think of a recent situation in which you were upset.
   Briefly describe the situation.

2. Identify the thinking triggered by the event which caused you to be upset by reflecting on what you were thinking and saying to yourself when the event occurred.
   I was thinking:

   I was saying to myself:

3. Be aware of the feeling associated with your thinking at the time and ask yourself how your thoughts made you feel.
   I was feeling:

   My thoughts made me feel:

4. Explicitly dispute the irrational thinking by providing evidence that what you were thinking is not true by questioning whether your thinking was based on reality.
   Evidence to dispute irrational thinking:

5. Identify more productive thoughts to take the place of your irrational thoughts.
   More productive thoughts:

The following is an example of how I used the process to work through a situation with a good friend.

Event:

> Michael didn't call to tell me he had gotten a job after a year of being out of work. We had been in regular contact and had spent hours discussing options. I had been sending him classifieds from the Internet for several metropolitan market areas. Then I found out from a mutual friend that he had started a job two weeks earlier.

Thinking:

> I was thinking he was inconsiderate.

Saying to myself:

> "How inconsiderate. He knows I'm concerned. Besides I'm wasting my time sending him want ads."

Feeling:

> I was initially annoyed and then became angry about how he was treating me.

How my thoughts made me feel:

> My thoughts moved me from annoyance to anger.

Evidence to dispute irrational thinking:

> Maybe what's really causing my upset is that I wasted my time the last two weeks reading the want ads for him. He must be in such a state—he's probably just totally self-absorbed right now and his sense of self-worth has been so eroded that he's doubting whether this new job is going to work out. He doesn't want to face the prospect of having to tell people he lost another job.

More productive thoughts:

> I'm happy that he found a job. I realize he was acting out of a sense of insecurity.

The process of explicitly disputing irrational thinking involves three forms of self-questioning for challenging irrational thinking. The first is to ask "Is it logical?" The second is to do a reality check by asking "Is it consistent with reality?" And the last way is to think about its usefulness by considering the consequences of holding onto these thoughts by asking "What results will it bring me?"

The idea is to talk yourself through the situation by moving progressively through the three types of arguments: Logical, empirical, and functional. To illustrate the process, consider "Doomsday" or "Woe is me!" thinking, the kind of irrational thinking in which you believe you deserve better than what life is giving you. Suppose you were about to go on a trip and got sick and had to cancel. So you're thinking "Bad things always happen to me."

(Logical) Is it logical?

> "Why should I think bad things only happen to me? Disappointments are part of life. They happen to everyone. Bad things happen to good people. It doesn't get me anywhere to wallow about things over which I have little control."

(Empirical) Is it consistent with reality?

> "Do only bad things happen to me? What are some of the good or positive things that have also happened to me over the last week?

(Functional) What results will it bring me?

> "What does expecting bad things to happen do for me? Does this kind of thinking make me feel better? Do I like feeling bad? Wouldn't I like to feel better? If I'm expecting something bad to happen all the time, I'll cut myself off from experiencing any joy in my life. If I change my thinking I might start to feel better."

Reconciling Acceptance and Change

There are some things about ourselves that we won't be able to change completely. However, creating an awareness about an issue in our lives can sometimes provide the impetus to alter our perception and bring about a shift. For example, consider the concept of guilt. Guilt can sometimes lead us to positive action, but generally it is a negative factor in determining our behavior. We would all agree that if a person's life is governed primarily by guilt this is not an ideal way to go through life.

Terry is someone plagued by guilt. She eventually decided to see a counselor to try to get her guilt under control. After some time Terry told me how pleased she was with her progress. She said, "I'm just one of those people who always finds something to feel guilty about, but now I am beginning to put my guilt in perspective. Although I haven't eliminated the guilt messages that are always in my head, I am able to turn the volume down so that it doesn't dictate my life. I'm able more and more to choose not to focus on it, but I think it will always be there with the potential to cause me pain. In accepting myself, I accept that the guilt is part of me. By accepting it, I can reduce its impact on my life."

On the change continuum, Terry may have moved as far as she is capable of going. Elimination of the guilt messages may not be possible. Developing a checkpoint for recognizing the guilt messages serves to bring them into consciousness, allowing her to exercise some control. In her case, she has moved to the point of being able to keep the guilt from dictating her actions. I suspect this is an instance where she will require active practice techniques and conscious and deliberate action to internally monitor the guilt messages. By active practice techniques I mean explicit prompting strategies to keep the guilt from becoming the driving force for her actions.

An example of an active practice technique would be to consciously pay attention to her use of language. Specifically, she might become aware of saying "I should" or "I can't." She may even keep a record for a time to gauge how often she uses these words. If her use is prevalent, then she might make a plan to begin substituting "I choose to" for "I should" and "I won't" for "I can't." This strategy can serve as a tool to constantly remind her to affirm her right to choice. Saying "I choose to" and "I won't" instead of "I should" or "I can't" helps to affirm your right to choose. "I can't" implies being unable, being controlled by some outside force; "I won't" takes responsibility and affirms that the decision belongs to you. This is only one example; there are many potential action plans once Terry identifies something tangible that can serve as a signal to redirect her thinking. The following affirmation may also be helpful.

Life is an opportunity not an obligation.

–B.L.

Some behaviors most would agree are desirable, such as being able to affirm our personal boundaries, stand up for what we believe, and express our needs and feelings. To be effective in the workplace and in personal relationships, these are highly desirable ways of behaving. To develop intimate relationships, it's important to be able to express our desires, needs and feelings to foster a climate of mutual vulnerability requisite for intimacy to develop.

We probably all know someone who has the positive characteristics of being very caring and considerate but also refrains from initiating any response that is likely to illicit confrontation. They protect themselves at all costs from being exposed to potential anger and rage. It is not unusual for those who are very considerate of others to pay more attention to helping others get their needs met than to mutually asserting their own needs.

Many of us confuse not expressing our needs with being considerate. We grew up being told things were "not polite" and that we were "being inconsiderate." So-called politeness is often a failure to validate our own needs in the guise of genuine consideration for others. Paying attention to our body signals can help us learn to weigh meeting our own needs with concern for others. These signals of body tension could be a churning stomach, facial muscles freezing, breathing faster, or a headache. The body often reacts more quickly than our intellect when we have been conditioned to think we are doing the right thing. Our body knows and sends out a warning message to give attention to our needs.

Even though a behavior is ineffective, it has both positive and negative consequences for the person. The positive side of not asserting our own needs is protection of our inner comfort. The advantage is that it appeases others and avoids conflict. The immediate consequence of allowing individuals to avoid or escape anxiety-producing conflicts is very reinforcing. People are often encouraged to be obliging by others who praise them for their selflessness, for being a good friend or child, or for being subservient and generally agreeable and not causing problems for others.

Some of the negative consequences associated with not validating our own needs can include not getting what we want or need, experiencing feelings of inadequacy, or getting angry at others for taking advantage, often leading to passive aggressive behavior. Unable or unwilling to express our feelings of resentment or anger directly can lead to dealing with our aggression in subtle and indirect ways, allowing us to maintain a facade of kindness and consideration.

If you tend to take a nonassertive stance, your behavior when a conflict or problem situation arises will often take the form of two different types of denial: Denying your own needs, or ignoring your needs. In both cases your response is to do nothing. In the first case you choose to forget about your own needs and satisfy the other person's needs. In the second case you pretend nothing is wrong, failing to acknowledge that a problem exists. In either case, you allow others to behave in ways that show no regard for your needs. The typical behavior mode is to either surrender or flee.

In the long run, a person who is frequently denying or ignoring his or her own needs may come to feel a growing loss of self-esteem and an increasing sense of hurt and anger. It can be a double-edged sword in that not only do you fail to get your needs met, but you feel bad about yourself as well. If this tension in constantly suppressed, somatic problems can develop such as headaches, backaches, stomach aches, or even depression.

To increase your awareness, you can begin to notice whether you are keeping an unwritten internal log of what you let the other person "get away with." If this is happening, you are likely to throw up such incidents to the person at a later point. This is a signal of unfinished business. Often we fail to assert our rights and needs because we are afraid it will negatively impact a relationship. Take, for example, someone who frequently borrows money from you and fails to pay it back. If you do not ask for repayment, you may find that unexpected barbs float into your conversations with the person, or that you avoid the person when you think he might ask you for money, or you find yourself lying about having any money. You have taken on some passive aggressive behaviors to deal with your resentment and the relationship certainly is negatively affected. The point is that failing to let the other person know that you feel violated often shows up in other ways alerting you to the fact that you have suppressed some negative feelings.

If you don't do anything, letting your silent resentment toward another person fester, it can spur displacement of hostility onto an innocent party. For example, let's say your boss has known about a deadline but let the work sit around for several days before giving it to you. The boss is now demanding that you meet the deadline. You are angry but you say nothing. Instead you come home from work and respond angrily to your son for something insignificant. This is not to say that you should always express resentment. Sometimes, if there is a lot at stake, it's better to remain silent and reduce the symptoms of the resentment. One way to deal with your anger is to change what you say to yourself. Another way is to refrain from making the other person wrong, putting your energy instead into making the situation better.

Sometimes there is a "hidden bargain" operating. I sacrifice some important right or preference expecting you to do something explicit in return, but I don't tell you what I expect in the exchange. A classic example is the employee who wants a promotion but instead of directly asking for it becomes a workaholic expecting that the employer then cannot possibly refuse the promotion. If the person doesn't get the promotion, he or she feels abused and used. Learning to go inside and ask yourself if you are operating on the basis of an unexpressed or assumed expectation can help you to identify your hidden bargains.

A similar situation typically crops up in intimate relationships when we have an implicit expectation that our partners will return our acts of good will and affection. When there is a hidden price tag attached to our kind acts toward our partner and we expect a "return in kind" for our investment, our partner will sense this contingency and interpret the behavior as ingenuine. He or she will invalidate the behavior if it is not unconditional. Operating on the assumption that your partner's role in life is to take care of your needs only sets you up for continual disappointment. If instead both individuals in the relationship are capable of getting many of their needs met independently, then each partner is more likely to be happy with the other. By taking care of their own needs they avoid a situation in which each is expecting the other to make his or her life happy.

I'm advocating paying attention to your inner signals that inform you when you are acting against yourself. What happens is that your new awareness opens up behavior possibilities that may have been previously blocked. This in principle is very different from following a prescription for a specific behavior change, for example, trying to learn to state your intentions. Although, when you have a new way of seeing things, this may lead to a behavior change. So it's not following a prescription to do this or do that, rather it's allowing your awareness to inform your practice.

Those who are typically nonassertive know that they act this way to maintain their own comfort level. They are usually quite aware that they fail to assert themselves because they don't want to have to deal with rejection, disapproval, or other confrontational or aggressive behavior from others. It can also be the case that a person espouses a nonconflict philosophy and is actually at peace with this way of behaving. If this is the case, and the person is not in denial, acting in passive aggressive ways, or feeling inadequate or angry, then there is no need to look further at the behavior. However, more often individuals who refrain from asserting themselves experience negative emotions, either directed at themselves or at the other person, or both.

If you evaluate your behavior pattern and determine that you don't want to accept the consequences of your current nonassertive behaving, you basically have two choices: Change your behavior, or don't change your behavior and cope more effectively with the consequences. Thus your action can be either proactive or reactive. If you decide that it's your natural way to refrain from asserting your opinions, desires, or feelings, you may choose not to expose yourself to potential or imagined conflict. By choosing not to change your initiating behavior, then your response will be reactive, dealing with the consequences of not expressing your needs. Now for some this may involve an awareness process to get in touch with their feelings because they may have convinced themselves that they don't feel angry or frustrated, that it's OK not to get their needs met or to be ignored. To get in touch with what's happening when you act nonassertively, you can begin paying attention to the feelings aroused by asking yourself questions like: Am I angry at the other person? Am I frustrated with myself? Am I resenting not getting my needs met?

So what you change is the way you deal with or cope with the consequences. For example, if you choose not to express your needs and become angry at the other person for asserting his or her needs, then you can try to disperse the anger by utilizing coping strategies to minimize the effects of the stressful situation. You can use physiological strategies to help deal with the physical reactions the body has to stressful situations such as relaxation techniques or working off your anger by some physical exertion. Or, you can use a more cognitive approach by engaging in anger control tactics such as self-talk and affirmations to cope with the anger symptoms. For example, you could repeat to yourself "I don't have to prove myself." Or, you can use visualization techniques and try visualizing the person in a very unpleasant situation. Whether you use physiological, cognitive or behavioral strategies, or some combination, you engage in some coping strategy to address your anger and move out of it. You don't try to change your nonassertive way of behaving because it would feel too unnatural and put you in conflict situations; instead you accept your nonassertive behavior and the resulting consequences and work to develop more effective coping strategies. You protect your inner comfort, but you also accept that there are side effects attached to the behavior and attempt to cope better with them.

If on the other hand, you decide you need a more proactive approach, then you attempt to change your nonassertive behavior. Many people may simply not know how to act otherwise because they have not had the opportunity to learn alternate strategies and need to engage in active practice techniques to try unfamiliar behaviors and begin to learn new ways of responding. Learning to express your needs, thoughts, and feelings clearly and directly without judging, dictating, or threatening will take some practice.

The most effective assertive responses are nonjudgmental, take a clear stand, and state personal needs. When a conflict situation occurs, the assertive response is to confront the situation directly. Appropriate effective responses could take any of the following forms:

- Simply stating your needs (I need to leave by 3:00.)
- Making your own intentions clear (I intend to apply for the new position, too.)
- Expressing your feelings without blaming (I was disappointed when you didn't call because I wanted to see you.)
- Describing the impact of the other person's behavior (When you are going to be late and you don't let me know I worry.)
- Making your position clear (This is really important to me.)
- Taking a stand (I am not willing to do that.)
- Actually requesting a behavior change (I would like you to tell me when I do something you don't like.)

Learning to clearly state your intentions in a conflict situation can help set the boundaries for what you are willing to do, as in the following example: "I don't intend to punish myself over making that mistake that upset you, but I do intend to be more careful in the future." It communicates that while you do feel remorse, you're not going to let another person's attempt to instill guilt dictate your behavior.

PERSONAL EXERCISE

Recognizing Powerless Language

One way to begin to look at whether you are hedging on expressing your needs is to notice your speech patterns. Chances are you're not affirming your rights, wants and needs if your messages are couched in "powerless language."

Ask yourself:

• Do I hedge my requests? Do I tend to say?:

"I *don't suppose* you would consider…?"
versus
"I *want* you to consider…"

"I guess I'd like to…" versus "I need to…"

• Do I tag on questions to seek approval?

"It's time we got started, *isn't it?*"

"…, *don't you think so?*"

• Do I preface my opinions with disclaimers?

"I probably shouldn't say this but…"

"I don't have much training in this area, but…"

The list of personal entitlements below can serve as affirmations to continually remind you of your human rights.

Personal Entitlements
1. I am entitled to be treated with respect
2. I am entitled to say no and not feel guilty
3. I am entitled to make mistakes
4. I am entitled to experience and express my feelings
5. I am entitled to fulfill my needs
6. I am entitled to take time and think
7. I am entitled to change my mind
8. I am entitled to do less than I am humanly capable of doing
9. I am entitled to ask for what I want
10. I am entitled to feel good about myself

Summing Up

So it isn't that I don't intentionally try to change a behavior that isn't getting me the results I want to a more need-satisfying behavior, but it's the process of being intune with the feelings generated by the "ineffective" behavior that serves as the impetus for the personal change effort rather than someone else's prescription for change. This doesn't mean that I won't benefit from others' suggestions of strategies for change, only that the decision to change comes from an internal motivation to address negative (i.e., self-defeating) emotional counterparts (i.e., resentment, guilt) of a behavior. Also one takes into account his or her own beliefs and predispositions and makes a choice accordingly. You don't take someone else's judgment about a behavior to be your truth. In other words, being assertive is not inherently better than being nonassertive. It's not as important whether you learn or don't learn more assertive ways of behaving, what's important is the heightened consciousness about how the consequences of failing to assert your needs are manifested.

Reconciling Force and Flow

My youngest sister said once during an emotional upheaval while I was in my usual consoling role, "You're so lucky—you were just born laid back." It was one of those "It's easy for you to say" comments. My immediate reaction was to take offense at this comment, thinking does she really think my behavior just happens, that there is no intentionality? I thought, isn't this interesting I've spent 20 years working on myself to get to this place and she thinks I'm just lucky! The way I saw it was that I make a conscious choice to put things in perspective, not to get caught up in "Woe is me" thinking. For me, this translates into perpetually asking "How bad is this really?" and "Relative to other things which could happen, how catastrophic is it?" as a guard against "awfulizing" a situation.

Although I was taking issue with my sister's notion of being born laid back, I recognize that we do have basic predispositions toward certain behaviors. Each of us is predisposed to act in certain ways and this natural predisposition facilitates certain ways of behaving and inhibits other ways of behaving which might be preferable or more effective in particular situations.

While the process of questioning and self-reflection allows me to understand what's happening for me and generally keeps me from judging, it can also serve to allow me to swallow some hurt feelings that I need to deal with. A strategy which is generally effective can be counterproductive when coupled with old defense patterns. In my case, it's the protection from dealing with another person's anger, no doubt stemming from parents who were prone to ranting and raving, that sometimes keeps me from expressing a feeling. So recognizing my own projections is important but it's also important to be able to allow myself the right to have negative feelings, to be able to say "I'm angry," especially when someone has infringed on my personal boundaries. This is a close call for me and is always difficult; it may never become easy.

This is where I go back again to the idea of force versus flow. I know for me there is this constant need to push myself to discuss a feeling or engage in a confrontation. My belief has changed and yet the corollary behavior seems always to be an effort. Now if I stop trying or let go of the effort I revert back to my old pattern of feeling bad and not being proactive. However, does this mean that I really haven't changed my belief?

Does this mean that my thoughts are thoughts of fear and so they inhibit my behavior? At some point do talking about my feelings and confronting become my natural way of behaving so the effort eventually diminishes? Does the effort to force being in tune with my feelings ever become a more natural flow? If we try to change our actions to behave in ways we perceive to be more effective, do these new behaviors ever come to feel natural?

There are several levels of dealing with one's feelings. One level is at the input where we check to see if we're adding our own baggage to the way we are interpreting another person's behavior. Another level is more proactive and that's where we are able to talk about our feelings at times other than when we are provoked by a situation. I seem to be more successful at the level of not letting my feelings escalate to catastrophizing them and less successful at the level of initiating an expression of my feelings. So my desire to change continues. However, I'm gratified that my current behavior does represent considerable progress on the continuum represented by the two extremes, from not being in tune with my feelings to being in tune and acting in harmony with my feelings.

We operate on the assumption that thought and feeling are separate. This position is exemplified by old adages like "Trust your gut feelings" versus "Think before you act." But it is our thoughts, our way of attributing meaning, our interpretation, that incites the emotional counterpart of a thought. What would represent arrival at the place I want to be would be a state of unity, where the discord between thought and feeling, "head and gut" was dissolved. At this point in my personal growth development I can only imagine what this would be like. In fact, I'm not even sure I can fathom it!

Summing Up

I'm choosing to think the effort will subside. I'm also willing to accept it's hard for me to do this and leave it at that for now. Hence, my personal reconciling of force versus flow. I accept that it takes a conscious effort until I have sufficient experience to replace the old ways of doing, until I have repatterned my memory cells. Because I believe that dealing on the feeling level is the path to creating intimacy in our relationships, establishing trust and forming emotional bonds, I make a conscious attempt to go against my natural way of acting, my predisposition to "stay in my head." I'm trusting that my comfort level will increase over time.

Reconciling Coping and Denial

I am using the term coping to refer to an appropriate reaction to a disturbing situation, or an anticipated difficult situation. It is a natural act of protection, a way of behaving that helps us survive and minimizes our vulnerability to another person or to a circumstance. Self-talk is an example of a coping strategy that can help us deal with an actual or anticipated stressful situation. Basically, we "talk ourselves through" an anticipated stressful situation by using self-statements to prepare ourselves for the situation, during the encounter, and as we feel the experience of being overwhelmed. In other words, we use our internal verbalizations to monitor our stress. Using affirmations is another example, such as repeating a phrase like "No one else can control me."

The difference between coping and denial can be a very fine line. Often coping and denial look the same. Sometimes what is a healthy coping skill for one person is denial for another. Or, what begins as a shortterm coping mechanism may evolve into longterm denial. What starts out as our way of getting through something can evolve into denial if it overruns its course. For example, you may sleep a lot when you're depressed or when you have suffered a loss. You are mentally exhausted and this exhaustion translates into physical exhaustion so that you actually do need more sleep. Sleeping more also gives you less waking hours to feel the pain. You know that you are sleeping an excessive amount and you accept that for the time being that is what you need to do. However, beyond the point of healing, and this will be individually defined, this excessive sleeping turns into a lack of effective coping which is the definition of denial. Coping, or getting by in a way that denies there is something that you need to look at or work through, is denial. Failing to accept reality is also denial, as is considering only your interpretation of reality.

Sometimes we develop coping skills for dealing with people who set us off. You know those people who seem to know just what buttons to push! We have learned when to stay in the game, when to fold and when to accept a stalemate. Sometimes these skills serve us well and keep us from being reinjured. Sometimes it's best to just let things be. But sometimes our ways of coping keep us in denial and prevent us from breaking through barriers. We may cope by avoiding some people all together, by staying away from particular situations, or by engaging in uncharacteristic behavior with certain people.

Although I seem to have dealt with the control issue for the most part, when it comes to dealing with my mother I find I often succumb to her unreasonable expectations. I'm still trying to please her, take responsibility for her being happy. Though I know my compliant behavior reinforces her controlling behavior, the consequences of provoking her wrath are ever imprinted on my memory slate. My way of coping with my mother is to do what I think it takes to keep her from becoming upset, even though this often means being nonassertive when I would normally be assertive when dealing with unreasonable expectations or reactions of others.

In my thought process I rationalized that because I empathized with the hard life she's had, the many sacrifices she's made as a mother and the disappointments she's endured, I should just ignore her behavior. I forgive her for her behavior partly because of her life experiences and partly because of my belief that she could not change; her ways are too ingrained. But my belief that she was not capable of changing served as a self-fulfilling prophesy. I felt powerless to effect change in her behavior and because I felt powerless I disempowered myself to change my behavior.

However, I've discovered that when I changed my behavior in dealing with her, she was able to change. So now I state my needs, make clear the boundaries for what I'm willing to do, and voice when I feel hurt or angry when her behavior infringes on my rights or disregards my feelings. I have found that she will listen, and over time does reflect on the feedback she gets from me and does change her behavior to more respectful behavior. This is another example of holding an irrational belief which inhibits more effective behavior. In fact, I had dual faulty beliefs operating, the first that she could not change and the second that she somehow had a right to mistreat others because of her sacrifices and disappointments in life.

What on the surface appeared to be a simple matter of confronting and asserting was much more deeply rooted. What I chose for years to label as empathy, forgiveness and acceptance kept me on a course of denial and avoidance of my true feelings of hurt, anger, and resentment. Until I chose to deal with it, I continued to be exposed to abusive and hurtful behavior.

Sometimes the ways we cope are effective strategies for protecting us, but other times they prevent us from taking the necessary risks to be vulnerable and break through barriers that prevent more meaningful interactions with others. The following quote cautions us not to get too comfortable in our coping.

> *Remove the rock from your shoe rather than learn*
> *to limp comfortably.*
>
> —STEPHEN PAUL

Summing Up

To return to the reconciling, sometimes we need to let go and let be, to surrender. However, we also need to find a balance so that "limping comfortably" isn't our predominant way of being. What we're balancing is protecting our own inner comfort with the courage to venture out of our safety zone with risk-taking actions to challenge what we have accepted as reality.

Reconciling Projection and the Past

Often we react to a situation based more on our past emotional experiences than to the reality of the present situation, leading to an irrational response. Rebecca's case is an example. For her, having her opinion challenged is perceived as a personal attack. Because she feels personally attacked, she counterattacks and subjects the person holding the opposing point of view to an abusive tirade berating he or she for having such a ridiculous opinion. In her case, feelings of powerlessness and personal attack stem from her adolescent years when she would constantly argue to no avail with her unyielding father about religion and other issues. Discussing an emotionally-charged issue still triggers these old feelings of powerlessness thus fueling an angry response.

The feelings of powerlessness and personal attack she experienced as an adolescent arguing with her father resurface whenever someone presents an opposing viewpoint. This is an example of irrational behavior stemming from the feeling of powerlessness. In this case, her reaction has very little to do with the other person's behavior. She reacts to the present with emotions linked to childhood experiences with a significant caretaker. The point is that we often evaluate the behavior of others through our own screens which filter what we are seeing. Here it's the screen of past experience—a simple statement of a different viewpoint when filtered through her past experience screen gets interpreted as an attempt to gain power and control and Rebecca sees the person expressing the opinion as an enemy. The real enemy is the feeling—one of helplessness.

> *We must look at the lens through which we see the*
> *world, as well as the world we see, and understand*
> *that the lens itself shapes how we interpret the world.*
>
> —STEPHEN COVEY

In Rebecca's case it will take a reframing of the situation to enable her to reinterpret the opposition and acknowledge the other person's right to defend a position. As an intermediary step, it may be necessary for her to engage in some anger or stress control strategies while embarking on the more longterm process of examining the feeling of powerlessness. Paying attention to the surfacing of the angry feelings can serve as the signal to engage in self-questioning. Rebecca might inquire within by asking herself questions like: What is my anger about? What's really at stake here? What do I seem to have to prove? Why is it important to win this argument? What assumptions am I making about this person?

Summing Up

Specific interventions which help gain immediate control in a potentially explosive situation are useful, and sometimes necessary tools. However, they will not take the place of the self-reflective process necessary to eventually transform the belief driving the behavior. In the example of Rebecca's feeling of powerlessness, the belief might be that I have to prove that I am right to have power. Or, I am not worthy unless I can convince others that my opinion is valuable.

PART III

Creating Your Personal Pathway

The Action Stage

Chapter 8

Repositioning and Moving into Balance

I use the term "repositioning" to connote the idea of changing our perception by "moving out of" our old position, or creating a new position. It's our personal framing that shapes how we attribute meaning to our experiences. If we are able to move out of our limited perspective then we can begin to see new ways of interpreting a situation.

Often we need to change the vantage point from which we view a situation to awaken ourselves to the realization that our frame of reference has trapped us into a limited perspective of how things are. By challenging ourselves to think in a different way we can attempt to assign a new meaning to the situations that confront us.

If we reflect on our own past we can find an event such as losing a job or ending a relationship that seemed awful when we experienced it, but as we look back on the event now, we see that it was an invaluable turning point. In losing the job, the change may have provided the opportunity to reassess your interests and to move into a much more enjoyable position. By leaving the relationship, you had the chance to develop another relationship that has been far more rewarding.

By repositioning a seemingly negative event we can, as the saying goes, see that "every dark cloud has a silver lining." Repositioning means to grasp the opportunity by attuning ourselves to the positive potential in any situation. When we reposition, we look for the opportunities to learn and grow in any situation.

Some helpful repositions include: Repositioning fear as challenge, repositioning conflict as energy, and repositioning attack as cry for help.

Repositioning Fear:
Moving from Foe to Friend

Fear can be defined as excitement without the breath. Fear creates energy, and that energy can be rechanneled so that we see the challenge not just the threat. If we can reposition the same emotion as excitement, we empower ourselves to move into the fear. If we can make this perceptual shift, then fear can become the energy to face a threatening experience with enthusiasm and successfully meet the challenges facing us.

Fear is often the fear of rejection, or negative evaluation from others. We fear that if they perceive our anxiety then they are evaluating us as a weak person. If we do something careless or impulsive then we fear others are evaluating us as careless and incompetent. We often expand our fear by believing that these negative evaluations by others are permanent and can't be changed. We engage in *always-never* thinking, believing that others will always see us as ineffective and incompetent, and that we will never be accepted. We fear the slightest mistake, as it may worsen opinions others have of us.

This type of thinking promotes a kind of negative self-watching where we are constantly concerned about our performance. Learning to refrain from rating, judging and evaluating ourselves, can help us put others' evaluations of us in perspective. If we become preoccupied with others' negative evaluations, we can actually cut ourselves off from perceiving and accepting the positive and supportive evaluations that others in fact may be making.

When we can detach ourselves from the outcome of our efforts, we can stay in the present and enhance our enjoyment in what we are doing. Letting go of our attachment to outcomes is also a facet of judgment in that we don't let a situation we cannot control effect our evaluation of our performance.

The judgment of others does not disturb me
when I know who I am.

—LAO TZU

∽

Before we can address fear, we have to be able to recognize it. The aim is not to eliminate fear or deny it, rather to be cognizant of the fact that fear is governing our actions. Courage is putting your fear in a realistic perspective by acknowledging it, considering the alternatives and choosing to function in spite of the fear.

Courage is not the absence of fear; courage is acting
when you do feel fear.

—SUSAN PAGE

∽

So the first step is to identify your fear and pay attention to it. Once you can raise the fear to a level of awareness, you recognize that you can act in the face of fear. In order to bring fear to the surface you have to become acquainted with your disguises for fear. Every organism has a built-in response to fear. A deer will stand motionless, a chameleon changes color, and a cat arches its back and hisses. We each have our automatic responses to fear that may not be at an awareness level. In my case, I am aware that one of the behaviors I use to disguise a fear of intimacy is to put up my intelligent disguise. As long as I am involved in indepth and complex explanations with people, I don't have to get personal. Or, I get intense and serious and want to talk about things and analyze them, in lieu of simply experiencing them. If I can let go of my need to get to the bottom of the matter by pressing for an explanation and pushing for closure, then I am able to let the feelings play out.

For some, their protective shield is to be funny, laugh everything off, or to be controlling, or to be charming. A person's disguise for fear is usually a positive trait that can serve the person well. If your tendency is to laugh away your fears, you are likely to be a genuinely funny person and a pleasure to be around. So the idea is not to abandon your sense of humor; only to become aware of the times you use it to mask a fear.

I am not advocating that we reject our disguises; our disguises are our natural defense system. I am advocating that we look at our disguises by engaging in a self-questioning process that allows us to examine if we are letting an underlying fear drive our behavior.

PERSONAL EXERCISE

Bringing Your Fears into Awareness

Try this exercise to bring your fears to an awareness level.

1. Give several responses to the phrase:

   "I am..., I play...."

2. Now try to identify what fear may be underlying your behavior(s).

   For example, "I am capable, I play dumb." In this scenario, it might be that I want to be liked and I'm afraid if I appear to be too smart I may be rejected.

Questions for Self-reflection:

- Is my reaction disguising a fear I have?

- What might I be trying to avoid?

- Is there something I would rather not look at?

- Am I denying a feeling?

Some maintain that there are really only two feelings, one of fear and one of love. A feeling of discomfort is embodied in the emotion of fear while a feeling of comfort is embodied in the emotion of love. All of our negative emotions are renditions of fear, or fear-based.

When we label an emotion fear, then we tend to back away from whatever is causing the fear. We try to get rid of the fear. Fear is what keeps us acting in familiar ways. Fear keeps us hanging on to our old ways, resisting change. We fear what might happen if we venture out of our comfort zone and break out of our usual patterns to allow a different approach to emerge. We surrender to the urge to stay in our familiar zone by suppressing the fear.

This struggle with fear and denial is a familiar struggle to all of us to some degree. We tend to hide our true feelings from ourselves and from the people around us. Some of us hide our sadness, some our fear, some our anger. We are afraid to allow ourselves the experience of anger. We do this because of fear, fear of rejection, disapproval, or punishment. We think we have to hide our true selves to be safe, to be protected. Many of our behaviors are actually childhood adaptations to pain, the things we learned to do to make the pain go away. We learned to ignore our bad feelings through distraction and denial. If we are able to lay down our masks and break through our assumed roles, we can begin to connect with our pain and anger. Because we fear that what is inside of us is dark and ugly, we repress our emotions. But if we have the courage to wrestle with our fear, we can learn to become real.

Repositioning Resentment:
Releasing Yourself of the Burden of Resentment

Sometimes our pain causes us to lash out at others, a primal cry for attention. It's our best attempt at the time to stop the pain. Eventually the pain subsides but the residue is resentment. We only sustain the hurt and remain in darkness as long as we hold resentment in our hearts.

If we can let emotional attachment and investment in the past dissolve, then we are able to free ourselves to move on. Allowing the walls of resentment to crumble softens the hardness in our hearts, permitting us to leave behind the resentment and move on with a generous heart.

To forgive doesn't mean to pardon, it means to let go. When you forgive the past, you unleash yourself from your attachment to the past. When you forgive, you give yourself the gift of freedom from the past. When you release another to go his or her own way, you free yourself to do the same. The process of giving yourself this gift of freedom is forgiveness.

When you forgive the other person, you do this not so much for the other person, you do this for yourself, for your own peace of mind. There is a second part of forgiveness and that is forgiving yourself for judging another. It was your judgment of the other person's action that caused the hurt. So you need not only to forgive his or her action, you need to forgive your judgment of his or her action. It's our judgment about the person that blocks the healing process of forgiveness. We believe that the person intended to inflict pain on us, but that person was only fulfilling his or her own needs. Perhaps it was at our expense.

Jack Kornfield, in *A Path with Heart*, sees forgiveness as a way to soften the heart and release the barriers to our loving-kindness and compassion. Forgiveness is simply an act of the heart, a relinquishing of the pain, resentment, and outrage that has been a burden to you. It is an easing of your own heart and an acknowledgment that, regardless of the amount of suffering you have endured from the deeds of another, you will not put another human being out of your heart. When you forgive it does not mean that you justify or condone harmful actions nor that you have to seek or speak to those who caused you harm. Forgiveness is something you do for your own sake, to carry the pain of the past no longer. The fate of the person who harmed you is irrelevant in the process of forgiving.

PERSONAL EXERCISE

Recognizing Judgment as Resistance

We often resist experiencing our own suffering by judging others and focusing on their injustice to us. The next time you find yourself being judgmental of another person, try this exercise to gain insight into what you may be resisting.

1. Notice that your attention is focused outwardly on the other person rather than inwardly on your own feeling.

2. Identify the *label* you have placed on the person's treatment of you.

   (For example, inconsiderate, unfair, hurtful)

3. Now ask: What is being judgmental keeping me from experiencing?

   (For example, if I label someone's behavior toward me as hurtful, then I keep myself from experiencing my hurt, i.e., the person is hurtful rather than I am hurt.)

Repositioning Loss:
Moving from Tomb to Womb

Loss is used here as a metaphor for feeling unwhole, that something has been taken away. Hence loss can be an obvious loss such as the death of a loved one or the break-up of a relationship. The feeling of being in limbo is also a loss. Not knowing whether something is on or off, being in a state of not knowing, a state of doubt, is a loss. Loss can also be developmental, such as menopause. A loss can also be a leaving behind what is familiar, moving into what represents a significant life change such as retirement, moving, or illness. In fact, any change represents a loss.

Processing loss and moving into recovery is both complex and longterm. First we have to identify what it is that we have lost. This means identifying everything that is entangled with the loss. When we get clear about what it is we have lost, then we can identify what is left. C. Edward Crowther reminds us that loss can serve as either a tomb or a womb, an ending or a beginning. If we see it as a beginning, then loss is learning.

The process of recovering from a loss typically involves moving through three stages. Though these stages are distinct, they are often overlapping. The first stage in the process is denial, a failure to accept what has happened. The second stage is anger that this has happened to you. The final stage is acceptance, allowing you to move on, preferably having taken the opportunity the loss provided to learn about yourself. Each of these stages is a normal part of the healing process. We interrupt this natural process if we neglect any stage. If we stay in denial and don't ever get to feeling the pain we may *go* on but we don't *move* on. A familiar example is the rebound relationship. Failing to go through the personal discovery process allowing the pain to melt into acceptance is likely to doom our future relationships as well. If we fail to get in touch with our anger, we may never come to know what the anger is about.

Although we can define stages of recovery, we cannot define the amount of time one should spend at each stage. Regardless of whether the loss is small or great, we move through these three stages. The difference is the intensity of feeling and the duration of the healing process. The greater the loss, the more intensely we feel each stage and the longer it takes to pass from one stage to another. We may move through the three stages in minutes for smaller losses, whereas for larger losses it can take years.

The healing or recovery process is just another dimension of the change process and hence progresses unpredictably, characterized by dramatic leaps forward and disappointing leaps backward.

Repositioning Conflict:
Moving from Threat to Opportunity

In discussing the nature of conflict, Thomas Crum, in *The Magic of Conflict: Turning a Life of Work into a Work of Art*, contrasts the western view of conflict as contest with the Eastern view of conflict as opportunity. This latter vantage point is recognized in the Chinese language where the character representing "crisis" is a composite of two characters, one representing danger and the other representing opportunity. In western cultures, conflict is viewed as adversarial, something to be avoided. In conflict situations, one dons armor and goes to battle, emerging as either the winner or the loser.

A new perspective is emerging from the new science which supports the position that conflict should not be viewed as something to be avoided or controlled, but as an opportunity for expansion and renewed life. Rather than fear conflict and try to contain it, this shift in perspective calls for exploring and actually expanding the conflict. We don't shy away from conflict, we embrace conflict as the gateway to higher forms of order.

The discoveries of modern science are converging with the ancient Taoist and Buddhist teachings to reshape our way of perceiving the world in general, and our perceptions about chaos and conflict, in particular. Both the new science and ancient wisdom present a model of the universe characterized by interdependence and relationships, not by fragmented pieces and separate entities. What's important is not the parts by themselves, but how they fit and work together, and the patterns they form.

Both these avenues point to an orderly, self-governing and self-organizing universe, replacing mechanistic models for explaining natural phenomena, organizational dynamics and human interactions with a more interconnected and unified worldview.

Fritjof Capra tells us that the two basic theories that have come out of the new physics embody the main features of the Eastern philosophical viewpoint. Quantum theory has abolished the notion of fundamentally separate objects and introduced the concept of participant observer, and has come to view the universe as an interconnected web of relationships whose parts are only defined as they come together, through their connections to the whole. These findings imply that everything each of us does has an impact on the world, not only our world but the universe. We don't look on from the outside; we're standing in the middle.

The significant similarity is that both the new science and Eastern philosophy view reality not as separate things but as a network of inseparable patterns. What had been viewed as opposites are now viewed as merely two aspects of the same reality. New physics presents another version of reality as a union of opposites. Rest and motion, mass and energy, time and space are all so mutually interdependent they form an interwoven continuum—a single unified pattern. One evolves into the other.

In this new perception of reality as boundless, where new realities are continuously emerging as patterns are reconfigured, conflict is not the opposite of harmony, each is an aspect of the same reality. In order to have harmony, we must have conflict. Before we can become whole, we have to allow ourselves to come apart, be unraveled. We can distinguish pleasure from pain, but we can't separate pleasure from pain. We can't know one without the other. We can't know harmony without conflict, nor can we separate harmony from conflict.

As Alan Watts pointed out, in the natural world the shoreline doesn't merely represent the separation of land and water but equally represents precisely that place where land and water touch each other. The shoreline joins and unites just as much as it divides and distinguishes. Lines in nature do not merely distinguish opposites, they also bind the two together in an inseparable unity. When we imagine two sides to be separate and unrelated, we are acknowledging their outer difference but ignoring their inner unity. Human beings are different in many ways, but their concerns and basic needs are the same. No matter what part of the world we live in, we have the same needs—to have meaning in our lives, to love and to be loved, to have the joy of relating with others.

The fundamental paradigm shift called for in these recent developments in the new science is the move away from concentrating on the parts to paying attention to the whole, and more importantly, to patterns created and relationship properties. In every domain we are beginning to explore the implications of this new way of thinking in which relationships become paramount and disorder and conflict are integral to rejuvenation and renewal. In international relations, in education and in business we are working to transform a culture of competitiveness to a climate of cooperation, honoring a spirit of collaboration.

In education, we are realizing that the curriculum has to be connected to the lives of children, including family, culture, and community. In business, we are trying to find ways to promote teamwork and collaboration in an atmosphere where change is welcome, conflict is embraced, and diversity is a resource rather than a liability. Some companies are beginning to encourage employees at all levels to challenge the status quo, to identify sources of conflict and let them rise to the surface. Many are applying this new science to business leadership and suggesting that we go as far as to stir things up, "roil the pot" and actually seek out those disturbances, conflicts, and contradictions that challenge and disrupt until, finally, things become so jumbled that a reorganization emerges giving birth to a higher order.

Our fear of the confusion and chaos experienced when in conflict causes us to instantly shut it down when it starts to appear. This shut down can either come in the form of overpowering, i.e., an aggressive response, or overstepping, i.e., an avoidance response. That is, we either move *in* or move *out* , but we don't move *through*. Instead of allowing ourselves to be uncertain and confused for awhile, to find our way through, and let go of the old ways of responding, we rush to closure, to "do something" to make the discomfort of not knowing what to do go away. The new science is suggesting that this chaos is a necessary and important stage in development. To break through our familiar cycles we need to allow ourselves to be overwhelmed, confused, anxious and afraid, not permanently, but for a time.

Conflict begins within. All conflict is inner conflict. Conflict is often about what we don't accept in ourselves projected outward. The vehicle for transforming the energy generated by conflict into a creative force originates at the core level of our relationship with ourselves, expanding outwardly to our interpersonal relationships, to relationships between groups, organizations, cultures and nations, to relationships between humanity and the Earth.

Any change creates conflict; all growth necessitates conflict. Hence, we can't change or grow without conflict. Conflict is an inevitable part of being. Seeking a middle ground between fleeing and fighting to win, involves a perceptual shift to search out the opportunity rather than retract from the threat; to expand rather than contract. So rather than "take cover" we strive to "uncover" the hidden opportunity.

When we view everything as interconnected, then we realize that we can't keep our personal hostility from spilling out of our own private energy sphere and into the collective energy of the universe. The more we have hostility and rage inside us, the more we live in a hostile world. When we join with another human being in a spirit of cooperation the energy permeates into the community, nation and the global village. If we want the world to be a loving and compassionate place, each of us has to become loving and tap our own compassion. The way to work for a better world is through the path of innerwork.

Modern physics speaks of "strange attractors" that organize and make sense out of turbulence and chaos. These attractors predict what type of order will appear in the midst of chaos. Just as the loose stones on a hillside are attracted to the valley, and pendulums swing until still, the worst personal or group turbulence tends, at least temporarily, toward resolution. Arnold Mindell posits that, in human systems, the drive toward balance, freedom and harmony may be an "attractor" in our individual development. A system's tendency to balance itself, or self-organize in modern scientific terms, however, can only partially be explained through causal reasoning. Change is also an incomprehensible and complex phenomenon; we don't know what creates change or when it will occur.

Concepts from field theory also contribute to our understanding of conflict. Fields are sometimes felt as forces, and in that sense can be likened to ancient Taoist beliefs in which the field is experienced as the Tao, a force running along "dragon lines," or "creases" in the universe. If you try to move out of these creases, you encounter resistance, hence the Taoist tradition to move along the lines of least resistance. Translated into field concepts, the parallel meaning is that we must balance inner feelings with sensitivity to outer situations. We are expressing a sense of these psychophysical fields when we say we can almost "feel" the tension between persons in conflict.

We live in a world where nations fear nations, races fear races, and the sexes fear each other. The fear that exists between nations is a macrocosm of the fear that exists between individuals. To diminish fear in the world, we have to diminish our own fears. Gary Zukav warns that when our path of learning is through fear we explore Earth with a sense of exploitation and domination rather than appreciation and cooperation. Being fearful produces feelings of depletion; being compassionate produces feelings of elation. The many expressions of fear take the form of rage, hate, resentment, envy, greed, guilt. Our task is to liberate ourselves from our own destructive energy forces and to rechannel the energy to create constructive ways of dealing with conflicts. We have to face into our fears, by moving into them, exposing and examining them, not denying and concealing them.

In *The Tao of Negotiation*, Edelman and Crain tell us that the person who negotiates from the Tao neither fears conflict nor tries to appease it, rather he or she accepts it with neutrality, as merely another form of energy that can either be used or diffused. To glean the many invaluable lessons our conflicts have to teach us, we have to learn to observe rather than condemn conflict.

Kenneth Cloke at the Center for Dispute Resolution suggests that we see conflict as a "request for communication." Often the purpose of anger is to get through to the other person so that person can finally hear what we are saying. Moreover, the largest part of anger is self-anger, redirected at another. It is our own fragile sense of self-worth that makes us want to counter with our own anger and aggression. When we are able to maintain our own detachment from the other person's anger and judgments about us and our behavior, we can "sidestep escalation," not responding in kind or running away, and explore the source of the anger. Responding with acknowledgment and acceptance rather than defensiveness, judgment, or denial helps us to hear an issue with concern for the other person, not as a criticism of ourselves.

Cloke suggests several ways in which conflict creates opportunity for enhanced communication, intimacy and understanding. These opportunities are relative to the person(s) with whom you are in conflict, yourself, the issue at hand, the interrelationship between them, as well as the nature of conflict itself. Conflict can allow for the deepening of empathy and intimacy with the other person(s) and for personal growth and self-realization brought about by a sense of empowerment when you are able to overcome your problems. Conflict can allow for a more comprehensive picture of the problem created by considering opposing points of view and can lead to a more satisfying solution. Having gained self-understanding and insight into your feelings and actions and those of others, and improved the relationship, you are better equipped to prevent conflicts in the future from escalating to the point where opportunity is masked.

If we can reposition conflict so that we perceive it not as a contest, rather as an opportunity for learning, growing and cooperating, we can use its energy creatively. Resolving conflict is not about being right; it's about acknowledgment and appreciation of differences. Apropos here is the saying that we learn much more from our enemies than from our friends.

The principles of organization underlying these revolutionary scientific discoveries point to a living, "learning" system, not a closed system. In such an open system, the evolutionary process that occurs at the level of the individual is the same process that occurs at each level of interaction between individuals. Our psychological universe expands as does the physical universe—both are open systems, not predetermined. Personal growth and self-renewal happen when we open up to experiencing the energy of conflict. By leaning into it and staying with the uncertainty of not knowing what to do and refraining from reverting to our familiar patterns, we allow ourselves to move into the conflict, go through it, and arrive at a higher place.

As we push beyond our personal boundaries and expand our awareness, we can begin to experience conflict as a burst of energy. The friction caused by this energy serves as a messenger revealing an opportunity to get unstuck. If we can let go of our need to be right or to win, we can transform the energy of our differences into creative energy. When we see conflict as merely an interference pattern of energies, not as a threat to our ego, or our existence, then resolving conflicts is not about being right; it's about acknowledging and appreciating differences and striving to discover a common ground. Rather than place blame and make judgments, we attempt to reveal underlying differences in experiences, assumptions and expectations. Conflict can spark new ideas if we remain willing to continue the dialogue, listening to each other in search of new understandings. Conflict can provide us with an opportunity for renewal if we are able to face the challenge with an open heart. Having an open heart means freeing ourselves from our judgments. Facing the challenge means being able to stay present with the conflict in a spirit of acceptance, simultaneously balancing acceptance of the conflict itself, acceptance of an other's vantage point, as well as self-acceptance of our right to differ. If we are able to experience the energy of engagement, it becomes possible to use the energy as a creative force.

By challenging our view of conflict and examining our defenses for warding off conflict and our arsenal of weapons for dealing with conflict, we can begin to experience conflict as a gift of energy. If we perceive conflict as an opportunity for learning, growing and cooperating, we can begin to trust in its power to recreate. Conflict can be the gateway to new beginnings. The challenge is to search out the opportunity, to ask what is the lesson to be learned by facing the conflict. Conflict teaches life's lessons; it's the stepping stone to tapping into our higher self.

The following guiding principles emerge from the new science and help us shape our ways of perceiving conflict.

Conflict is Natural
- Conflict is part of the natural order
- Conflict and harmony are two aspects of the same reality

Conflict is Merely Energy
- Conflict is an interference pattern of energies
- Conflict is not negative or positive
- Conflict provides impetus to channel energy to recreate

Conflict is Opportunity
- Conflicts can join and unite as much as they can divide and distinguish
- Conflicts are to be encouraged, explored, even embraced
- Conflict can move us to new levels

Personal Conflict is a Microcosm of World Conflict
- The path to diminishing fear between nations is through challenging our own fears
- Inner conflict and outer conflict are part of an interconnected web

As we expand our perception and heighten our awareness, we can begin to see conflict in a new light. Crum calls conflict "a gift of energy, in which neither side loses and a new dance is created." Similarly, John Heider also uses the metaphor of conflict as dance in advising us to recognize an encounter as a dance and not a threat to our ego or existence. He asserts that we should neither avoid nor seek encounters, but when encounters occur we should be open and respond by telling the truth.

> *The energy of our differences can produce a precious gift*
> *we could never have experienced alone.*
>
> —THOMAS CRUM

Resolving everyday conflicts at home or at work requires a willingness to understand the other side and to attempt to develop and communicate in a common language. As an example, let's say Jack, the hawk, and Sally, the dove, are caught up in a debate about war and peace. Instead of digging deeper into her own defensive trench trying to make peace the right choice, Sally moves off her position and inquires sincerely about the beliefs that lead Jack to his stand. Jack responds with "What I'm really interested in is security. I feel deeply about the health and well-being of my children. I want to see a world in which my children and my children's children can be secure and safe to grow up and be happy." And the commonality of thought between them is born—they both want a world that's secure and full of opportunity for future generations. By moving away from a right-or-wrong stance, they begin to understand each other, and to be understood.

There are lots of books out there telling us how to manage conflicts. They offer us "effective strategies" and "essential steps." They teach us the secrets to know how to get "win/win solutions," "win every negotiation," "get past no," and "get to yes." But conflict is not just about managing or strategizing, or necessarily resolving. Dealing with conflict is not only about learning conflict resolution strategies. It's about transcending solution-finding and getting to something much deeper. Resolving conflicts is much more pervasive than following a plan, step by step. A more holistic perspective is needed if we want to address conflict as an integral part of the stuff of life.

Trying to translate the new science and ancient Taoist teachings into ways to think about conflict and approach conflict resolution raises many more questions than it answers. Below are some of these questions I have been pondering.

- How do we work with the concepts of wholeness and interconnectedness in terms of conflict?

- If parts are only defined through their connections to the whole, how does that affect our notions about interventions?

- Do we really resolve conflicts by following sequential steps? by applying "conflict resolution strategies?"

- How do we shift from viewing conflict as a threat to perceiving conflict as opportunity?

- How do we "open up" to the opportunity conflict presents?

- How do we suspend judgment? honor diversity?
  accept different positions?

- How do we begin dialogue when we have a value clash?

- How do we seek out the lessons conflict can teach?

- What do we need to develop to face the challenge of conflict?

- How do we experience the energy of engagement in conflict
  to discover its creative force?

I offer that if we come from a place of "knowing" the possibility of harmonious resolution, then solutions avail themselves. If we can honor the *essence* of forgiveness then we will discover what it is we need to develop to face the challenge of conflict and realize the opportunity.

Unmasking the Opportunity in Conflict

Because all conflict is to some degree a reflection of inner conflict, identifying your part in the conflict can help you move toward resolution.

The next time you find yourself in conflict, ask yourself these questions.

- What did I do to contribute to the conflict?

- Am I doing anything to sustain the conflict?

- What is keeping me from moving "through" this conflict?

- Am I willing to move away from my position?

- What choice could I make to move toward resolution?

The following guided meditation is an exploration of the visual and physical sensations of being "at war." You may want to try this meditation to begin to reflect on a conflict you are struggling with by exploring "your inner terrain." This meditation may help you discover what you need to develop to face the challenge of conflict and what may be keeping you from moving through the conflict and experiencing the energy of engagement to discover its creative force.

Conflict Guided Meditation

Gently close your eyes.
    Let yourself settle into a comfortable position.

Take several deep breaths.
    Let every outgoing breath carry away any tension you
    might feel.

Become aware of the rhythm of your breathing.
    Allow yourself to become calm and receptive.

Begin to reflect on a conflict you are struggling with.

Gently allow a picture, a feeling, a sense to gather.
    As you sense this conflict, notice how it affects your body.
    Notice how it affects your heart.
    Notice how it affects your mind.
    Can you sense a barrier?
    Can you feel it? What is the feeling?

Can you see a barrier in your mind's eye?
    What does it look like?

Now ask yourself, what might the barrier be keeping out?
    What might it be keeping in?
    Is the barrier protecting something?
    What might it be protecting?
    Can you see your way around it?

Is the barrier keeping you from seeing or feeling something?
Is there something you need to look at?

Become aware of where your battles are being fought.
Where are your hot spots?
Sense them in your body.

Now ask: What is at war?

Become aware of how you have carried on your battles.
Be aware of how long the conflicts have been going on.

Is there something you need to let go of?

Gently, with openness, allow each of these
experiences to be present.
Simply notice them with interest and kind attention.

If you can, allow any barriers to dissolve.
Allow any walls to crumble.
Let your mind, body, and heart soften.

Feel the lightness in your heart as you let go.
Breathe quietly and let yourself be at rest.

Summon your inner guide to join you
at the peace table in your heart.
Ask for a symbol of peace to present itself.

And now, let your attention return to the present.

When you are ready, slowly open your eyes.

▼

Conflict in Intimate Relationships

In intimate relationships, conflict often occurs when our partner's behavior collides with our own interests and gets in the way of what we want. This is a major cause of conflict in relationships, with the typical response being one of denial of our partner's needs. When our expectations of our partners clash with reality, we often resort to weapons to help us support our illusions. Our arsenal of weapons includes criticizing, judging, threatening, denying, invalidating and analyzing our partner's behavior. We criticize by putting them down; we judge them to be bad, wrong, or inconsiderate; we threaten by giving them ultimatums for changing their behavior; we deny them by pretending they really don't mean it; we invalidate by telling them they really don't feel the way they feel, and telling them how they should feel; or we analyze them by explaining exactly why they are wrong. Engaging in any of these responses serves to diminish our partner's sense of self and support our own illusions.

We often convince ourselves that we know what our partner needs, usually without even realizing it. Frequently our assumptions are based on what we want our partner to be or to have so that our partner will meet our expectations. What this does in effect is replace our partner's needs with our own self-serving desires, typically leading to conflict.

Examining Assumptions about
Your Partner's Needs

Rather than assuming you know what your partner needs or what your partner should need, identifying your partner's needs in a conflict situation can help you move toward resolution.

The next time you find yourself in conflict with your partner, ask your partner these questions.

- What do you need our relationship to provide?

- What do you need as an outcome of dealing with this conflict to make you feel our relationship has been improved?

Often the messages we send communicate that only some of our partner's feelings and behaviors are valid. This is the same message we got from our primary caretakers—that only certain behaviors are acceptable, causing us to repress part of ourselves. When our partner refuses to accept our needs by denial and judgment, it perpetuates our sense of unwholeness. Only when we can be real and feel secure enough in our relationship to show our true selves, made up of both positive and negative emotions, can we become whole.

Negative tactics often become the weapons of love as an attempt to force others to be more loving. Instilling pain in the form of withholding attention, becoming distant, critical and blameful is a desperate attempt to get them to return to loving ways. The belief that hurting your partner will make him or her warm and responsive stems from infancy and is part of our stored memory about how to get our needs met. As infants we screamed and our mothers arrived on the scene to restore comfort. The instinctual cry as a response to distress is translated in adulthood into provoking others by being as nasty as possible until someone comes to the rescue. Even though this response typically only triggers a counteraggressive response, we persevere. This perseveration is a purposeful attempt at resolution. Freud coined the term "repetitive compulsion" to describe this tendency to repeat ineffective behaviors over and over again.

In addressing the issue of conflict and tension in love relationships, John Welwood takes a different tact. Feeling the pull of different tendencies inside us produces tension. While this tension is uncomfortable at first, it is the kind of creative tension that often gives birth to a new idea. He relates the story of a Zen teacher of archery trying to help his student learn how to stand with bow fully drawn and release the arrow spontaneously at the point of maximum tension, without any deliberate effort. He likened this process to snow falling off a bamboo leaf. The leaf keeps bending lower and lower under the weight of the snow until the snow suddenly glides to the ground by itself, without the leaf having exerted any pressure. He draws the parallel with intimate relationships continually leading to moments of crisis and tension. If we try to release the tension prematurely, this is like *trying* to shoot the arrow and we will likely miss the genuine resolution that could really propel us forward. Resting a while at the point of maximum tension, feeling and trusting the rawness that arises there is what he refers to as "balancing on the razor's edge." If we wait there in alertness, the leaf will bend low enough for the snow to fall off by itself, and the way forward can become clear.

At the beginning stage of a love relationship, we may at first try to resolve the tension and uncertainty by pitting different sides of ourselves against each other by trying to force a decision—should we run or stay? Welwood tells us that this leads nowhere because these alternatives are the product or our "busy oppositional mind," which is capable of grasping only one side of any polarity at a time. Such impossible choices only throw us into a state of ambivalence. Ambivalence is a vacillating attempt to choose sides, first one then the other, instead of letting both sides stay active until we find our natural equilibrium. Ambivalence is very different from balancing on the razor's edge, a state which calls on us to stay present with our sense of uncertainty rather than take sides in our inner debate. If we can give up our preconceived agendas about what *should* happen, then we may see how our fear is arguing us out of our love, or how our passion is trying to override our caution. We begin to "dance on the razor's edge" when we boycott this struggle, neither suppressing nor indulging either side.

If we give in to our urge to stay in our comfort zone by getting rid of our fear, we either fight against our fear or let it take over. If instead "we take our seat and face into our fear," we draw on a deeper resource within us.

If we suppress our anger, that only cuts us off from our feelings and makes us less present. Yet, if we just hold onto our anger, it becomes a rigid stance and creates distance. The whole person has both these sides to contend with. If we struggle to resolve these opposing points of view, we remain at an impasse. Recognizing these different parts of self without leaping to one solution or another leaves one feeling somewhat raw and shaky. The trick is to stay on the edge by leaning into it instead of resisting it by falling into some old pattern of blaming, or justifying, or denying. If we can accomplish this then we may be able to create an awareness that can open up the realm of possibilities.

Welwood believes that it is the love relationship that offers us an unparalleled opportunity to become our true selves, to become whole.

> "By teaching us to include all ourselves—courage and fear, cele-bration and pain, expansiveness and imagination—love helps us become both tough and tender at the same time. This strength that is also soft and gentle is the true child of the union of man and woman. Every couple struggling to learn to love partakes in the labor of this birth."

The success of a relationship is largely determined by how a couple handles their inevitable differences. Finding a compatible fighting style to deal with disagreement and anger is an important ingredient of lasting relationships. John Gottman has identified three styles of interacting that characterize successful marriages. He defines these three types of stable marriages as validating, volatile, and conflict-avoiding. What most ther-apists have in mind as the only way a marriage can work is the validat-ing style, in which each partner validates the others opinions and emotions, even though they disagree. When they fight, they are able to listen, acknowledge their differences and negotiate agreement without screaming at each other. They engage in dialogue, compromise often and calmly work out their problems to mutual satisfaction.

The two other patterns of successful unions represent very different styles of interacting. Volatile couples thrive on unfiltered emotional inten-sity. When they fight, they are full of angry growls; they fight bitterly, and even unfairly. While there are sudden ruptures, there are also romantic reconciliations. The passion with which they fight seems to fuel their pos-itive interactions as well. These couples can be more romantic and affec-tionate than most.

In conflict-avoiding working relationships, neither partner wants to make waves. Problem resolution in this style usually means ignoring the difference, one partner agreeing to act more like the other, or more often, just letting time take its course. Their agenda is to keep peace by minimizing argument and agreeing to disagree. In this more restrained style there are fewer swipes and caresses and they are also expressed less intensely. While some would find this style stifling, other couples experience it as a peaceful contentment.

The important point here is for couples to have a compatible fighting style, not to refrain from fighting. While anger and disagreement may lead to temporary anguish, it's healthy in the long run. The second point is that it is the rebalancing after the conflict that is critical, not necessarily avoiding the conflict, or how the conflict was addressed. All couples don't need to acknowledge, validate and compromise to maintain a successful relationship; other styles can be equally as effective. Furthermore, trying to force all couples into the validating mold has contributed to much of the failure in relationship therapy.

Couples who succeed cultivate an affirming story of their lives together. Warm memories about how they met, fell in love and made commitments are still vivid. They don't allow the story of their marriage to be infected with negativity. Successful couples also find a way to ride the storms of love by successfully coping with stressful situations. In her research with couples whose unions had thrived despite their inevitable rocky times, Susan Page found that a critical ingredient was their ability to hold onto the (sometime) distant memories of good times during the more difficult times. When feeling engulfed with pressures, resilient couples were able to band together and resist the urge to retreat into themselves and suffer alone. Part of feeling discouraged is the sense that you have always been depressed and that you will always be. Couples with lasting power are able to keep perspective and step back to see the big picture during the down times. They are able to draw on their inner confidence that good feelings will return and this provides comfort and keeps them going.

Chapter 9

Ways of Being for Moving into Balance

Principles for Moving into Balance

As I sort through all the principles, philosophies and ideas I have encountered, I think the most important learnings from my self-improvement excursion are related to the following concepts. Although these concepts are distinct, they are interrelated and sometimes indistinguishably intertwined.

- Control theory
- Projection
- Challenging irrational beliefs
- Choice
- Giving attention to feelings
- Nonjudgment

Of all the concepts and ideas I have been exposed to over the years I have identified six that have been meaningful counsel for me and help me to move into balance. By that I mean, these are the notions that have inspired much of my reprogramming of old tapes. These are the principles I seem to have integrated into daily practice. These are my prescriptions for "whatever is ailing me." When I'm feeling bad I can usually use one, or a combination, of these principles to figure out what I need to do. I'll give you my very simple and practical version of what each of these concepts means and why they are critical considerations for me.

Control theory posits that most of what we do is not a reaction or response to events around us. We are not controlled by external forces outside of our control, rather we control ourselves by forces that lie within. How we feel is not controlled by others or events. It is our nature to try to satisfy as best we can basic needs for survival, acceptance, freedom, power, and satisfaction. We control our own behavior by choosing to do things that satisfy these basic needs. All any of us do, think, or feel is always our best attempt at the time to satisfy the forces within us. And frequently, our best attempt is an ineffective solution.

From this basic theory stems the important message that although much of what we do is an attempt to control others, in reality we can control only our own behavior. Furthermore, if others are controlling us, then we're choosing to be controlled. From this theory also stems the assertion that we should not let others control us by the pain and misery *they* have chosen.

This is always a first checkpoint for me, to determine if I have allowed someone else to take control. While I want to empathize with another person's pain, I don't want to be drawn into supporting the misery the person chooses to deal with the pain. This concept also helps me determine if I am trying to control another person and helps me let go.

Pain is inevitable. Suffering is optional.
—M. KATHLEEN CASEY

～

The concept of choice is deeply imbedded in control theory. Life may have given me lemons, but I can choose to make lemonade or to suffer in misery. While I endorse the concept of "happiness is a choice," one may not be able to choose happiness at any point in time. Not choosing happiness temporarily can allow us to process grief, loss or disappointment. It can also help us make a plan to address our vulnerability to the situation occurring again. If there is a loss involved and the loss has been substantial, the recovery process will take some time. Feeling the pain, sadness and anger is part of the healing process necessary to get to acceptance and then to moving on. The amount of time it takes to make this transition will largely be a function of the intensity of the emotion involved. The important point is to move *into* choosing happiness over suffering.

Now, choice is also closely related to paying attention to and dealing with feelings as well as irrational beliefs. I may fail to allow myself to experience the pain, trying to *make* myself happy. Or, I may deny my anger due to an irrational belief that I should know better than to feel angry or that expressing my anger is always bad, or that I should be able to choose happiness, *now*. If my loss has been a divorce, and I really hold the irrational belief that I cannot live without the other person or that my spouse didn't have the right to satisfy his needs at my expense, then the belief will keep me suffering and inhibit me from choosing actions to end my suffering.

At an early stage of negative emotional feelings my internal monitor alerts me to try to get in touch with what is happening inside for me. This keeps me from revving up my negative emotional state. I take stock of whether I am being driven by a negative emotion. For example, if I start to think someone has taken advantage of me, is not appreciating me or is judging me in some way, my thoughts about that person are negative— How dare she treat me that way, how insensitive he is to my needs, what right does she have to judge me? and so on. When my inner dialogue is filled with these kinds of questions I feel violated. So if I feel violated, there must be a "violator." When my inner questions are focused on blaming others or projecting their intentions, I recognize that I am judging others by evaluating their behavior toward me as bad. Judging the behavior of others is a violation of one of my basic tenets. When I am judgmental rather than accepting, I become blinded and am unable to see others' perspectives or acknowledge their needs. If I continue in this vein, I become engulfed in a sea of negativity. I perpetuate in replaying the scene over and over in my head. Often signs of emotional stress appear, lack of concentration, headache, irritability, and shortness of breath. When I do this, I become resentful and angry, typically resulting in taking an aggressive action toward that person. Or, I may decide instead to get my resentment under control by repressing the feeling and going into denial. If I deal with my resentment by denying it, this keeps me from taking any action toward resolution.

So as long as I'm in a judgment mode, my behavior alternatives are likely to be either of two ineffective strategies, attack or denial. Now, if instead, I can revert to self-reflection, my internal questioning is characterized by questions like: "Did I make my needs known?" "Did I allow myself to be taken advantage of? "Am I accepting an other's judgment of my behavior in place of my own assessment?"

I also ask what old circuits are being sparked by the behavior. If I am able to identify old wounds as triggering my reaction it helps me to "take my feeling back" in a sense. That is, I remind myself that my hurt is deeply entrenched and it's my responsibility to be aware of this, not the other person's job to figure out what's going on with me. I spent several years being unhappy in my marriage waiting for my spouse to figure out what I needed. My belief was that if he really loved me he would just know when my feelings were hurt and that I needed something from him. I held the belief that if you have to ask for something it somehow diminishes the receiving. Recognize that old tape? "If I have to ask for it I don't want it." The process of my learning it's okay to ask for what you need was quite a discovery. I asked. I got. I felt much better! Not to mention how relieved the other person was to know what it was I wanted! It was really quite a surprise to find out the other person really didn't have a clue what I wanted and that he would gladly give it. My assumption that it was a deliberate withholding was all wrong. I was perpetuating my misery by holding onto a belief that did not represent reality.

The process of going inside and engaging in self-reflection helps me to see others' perspectives and consider their needs. It also helps me to monitor my hurt and to not accept the judgments of others. However, because my old behavior pattern was one of feeling hurt and withdrawing, I still have traces of these old memories to erase. So, my self-reflection is sometimes skewed with the tendency to rationalize, explain, or interpret rather than deal with my feelings. I use self-reflection to replace my old behavior as my way of addressing issues and concerns because for me this is more desirable than being resentful or trying to retaliate and punish others. I accept that engaging in this process may sometimes result in overrationalization because dealing with my feelings is still hard for me. I believe the self-reflective process is the key to making appropriate choices and offers the greatest potential to be at peace with my choices.

Paying attention to feelings and projection are also closely related. I need to be in touch with my feelings and allow them to surface before

I can evaluate whether my current feelings are primarily due to, or at least exacerbated, by my old wounds. Jung said our enemies and our lovers are projections or our dark side. Each person has a conscious self and a dark side which encompasses our unexpressed feelings and longings, our shadow. Beneath our conscious self lies the unconscious shadow, our hidden fears, weaknesses, longings—everything we don't accept about ourselves. Until we accept the unexpressed parts of ourselves, we're vulnerable to someone who expresses them.

Projection can also be projecting one's own values on another person. Whenever there is a value clash, a power struggle is likely to ensue as one person tries to impose his or her values on the other person. Now we're back to control theory. We're also probably dealing with getting in touch with feelings as well as judgment.

We tend to judge a behavior as good or appropriate based on our own comfort zone. We project our own intolerance for certain behaviors and consequently make a value judgment about the behavior of others. More simply stated, because we don't like a particular behavior we don't want others to act that way. We decide that they shouldn't act that way and we reject their behavior. Sometimes we may go even further to reject the person as well. This is another important lesson to learn, distinguishing between the deed and the doer. You want to communicate to others that while you may disapprove of their behavior at times, you still accept them. In other words, even though you may reject the behavior, you are not rejecting the person. This is the essence of acceptance.

We may decide that the person needs to change his or her behavior and even set about trying to help the person change. Trying to change others to act the way we would like them to act is just another facet of judgment.

Take as an example being verbally abusive. This is a definite taboo for me. I am particularly sensitive to verbal attacks and character assaults having grown up in a household where there were constant harsh flare ups. In addition, my education and training have made me extremely cognizant that self-acceptance can be very fragile and is adversely affected by negative evaluation. So, I have developed a personal interaction style in which I attempt to use the language of encouragement rather than the language of discouragement. I try to refrain from blaming, evaluating, diagnosing or offering prognoses.

The following story illustrates the point I am trying to make. A friend of mine will lash out at her significant other with such typical blaming phrases as "You should have known better", "What were you thinking!", "I can't believe you did that!". Or use the proverbial why questions with their more subtle implications of blame, "Why did you do that?", usually accompanied by the automatic body language of head shaking and the corresponding facial expression of disgust carrying the hidden message that only an inconsiderate fool would do that! However, after a few minutes of this type of harangue she calms down and can readily put the incident behind her. Her partner who never raises his voice accepts that this is the way she deals with her anger and manages to resurface unscathed. The incident came and went and there is very little residue. Now, because I judge this behavior to be unacceptable for me, I tend to project my own attitude about verbal abuse onto my friend and think that she should change her behavior. And yet, this verbal outburst appears to get them through their problem in a way that works in their relationship.

The lesson here is to learn to let go of your judgment and accept others' behavior even though it is in opposition to your beliefs and stretches your comfort level.

The most pervasive concept of all is the idea of judgment versus acceptance. When there is conflict, judgment is most likely involved. Being nonjudgmental is not evaluating something as good or bad by a universal standard; that is, applying the standard regardless of the circumstances or situation. Everything happens within a particular context; everything is contextually-bound. Nothing happens in isolation. Being judgmental is expecting people to act the way you would act. It is also judging them to be wrong or bad when they act in ways that are contrary to your beliefs. Judgment is also labeling, analyzing and evaluating.

When we shed the burden of judgment, we quiet the
turbulence of our internal dialogue.
—DEEPAK CHOPRA

Quieting the Mind and Body

Our mind is typically engaged in anxiety-producing thoughts which trigger the fight-or-flight response keeping our body in a state of arousal. Our body's other response is the relaxation response, a state of lowered arousal which diminishes many adverse symptoms brought on by stress. The secret of effectively regulating stress is to learn to cultivate the ability to experience inner peace. It is our perspective on things, our mental appraisal of external events, that determines our emotional tone and our level of stress. So the path to achieving optimal health and fostering balance and harmony is to learn to regulate our mental activity. Learning to control the mind does not refer to some automatic process like switching a light on or off as if we can turn on and off harmful thought patterns. Rather, it is a process of directing the activity of the mind. Control in this sense means that we are aware of and then exercise choices that affect our mental activity. We direct the mind away from patterns that create suffering and stress toward patterns that lead to inner peace and self-enfoldment.

In yoga tradition, the mind stands between, and yet at the same time connects, our most essential being with what is external. Through the activity of the thoughts and senses, we come to know and express ourselves in the world of experience. The analogy often used is that the mind is like a lake. The bed of the lake is our essential self, the water is the mind stuff, and the waves, currents and turbulence in the water are our thoughts, feelings and memories.

Managing Stress

Stress management can occur on two levels, at the prevention level or at the coping level. At the prevention level, stress inoculation attempts to minimize potential stressors so that we are "inoculated" against the harmful effects of stress. On the other hand, coping strategies for stress management attempt to minimize the effects of stressful situations so that we can cope more effectively with stress-producing situations.

Some techniques available to help manage stress produce a direct effect on the body. Such techniques help us deal with the physical reactions the body has to stress. Strategies that deal with the direct effect on the body are physiological and include diet, exercise, and relaxation. We all need to have some type of physiological coping strategy. Physiological stress coping skills that release the relaxation response include diaphragmatic ("deep") breathing, progressive relaxation techniques, and meditation. Progressive relaxation produces a deeper and longer-lasting state of relaxation than diaphragmatic breathing. It involves alternately making your muscles tense and then relaxed. The idea is to learn the difference between these two states so that you can better recognize tension in your body and use progressive relaxation techniques to achieve relaxation. Hypnosis and creative imagery techniques such as guided fantasy and guided meditations are typically included here as well. Visualization techniques set the stage for listening to your unconscious and use the creative power of your imagination. Such techniques can be used for relaxation, personal exploration, problem-solving, healing or self-change.

Managing Stress at the Mental Level

Many other methods and techniques have been developed to achieve mental balance and harmony. Developing a quiet mind is having a way of pulling in to yourself and creating a state of awareness. Deepak Chopra calls this slipping into the gap between our thoughts. Joan Borysenko calls it creating an observation point from which we can witness and let go of our old dialogues. John Welwood calls it returning to a state of simple presence, noticing our thoughts and then letting them go. Jon Kabat-Zinn calls it a process of deepening and refining our attention and awareness so that we come to realize our path of life is unfolding, moment by moment. They are all strong advocates of mindfulness meditation as the vehicle for creating such a state.

It is important to have a way to access the body's relaxation response, to be able to quiet the body and the mind. We need to find ways to catch ourselves in the act of constructing our familiar stories so we can make the shift from thought to awareness of what is immediately happening.

In our normal state, the mind is preoccupied with an inner dialogue which is an endless stream of thinking, providing commentary on our experiences. Our mind is a realm of metaphors, myths, and movies. The repetitive stories we tell ourselves about how the world works serve to perpetuate our automatic ways of interpreting the world. Although these stories are self-invented, fabrications of our minds, nonetheless they serve the function of putting our immediate experiences into our past experience framework, weaving our own tall tales. These stories in the background of our mind keep us locked in our judgments, assumptions and interpretations. Our self-created storylines wreak havoc in our lives by creating a mental picture of how things *ought to be* and keep us from experiencing how things *are*.

As we learn to listen in on the internal dialogue lingering in our mind, observing our thoughts and becoming more aware of our feelings and actions, we can begin to surrender automatic ways of interpreting our world. We have to keep attacking and challenging the repetitive thoughts that endlessly parade through our minds in order to open up to new realms of possibility. We need to be able to create a quiet mind, totally free from thinking, interpreting, and replaying the past.

One avenue is the practice of meditation which calms the body through the relaxation response and fixes the mind in awareness. Technically, meditation is an activity of attention and concentration, not relaxation. Relaxation is a by-product of meditation, much as it is of other focused activities such as athletics, dance, or sex. Meditation is a popular strategy, but any strategy that creates silence and takes you inside to a place of inner peace can precipitate the relaxation response. By returning to your inner self, you anchor the mind in awareness and stop the endless flow of noise and interference constantly parading through your mind.

Meditation can be any activity that keeps attention fixed in the present moment. You could also use the words introspection, stillness or simply quiet time. A meditation state grounds us in the infinite, allowing us to transcend our normal state of consciousness, surrendering to a higher awareness. When we block out everything but the focal point commanding our attention, we are in a meditation state. It is a state of deep concentration, in which we are totally engrossed, fully present.

Being able to relax the mind and access a place of inner peace and silence, allows us to tune into what is happening in the present moment.

To fix the mind in awareness, a focusing tool is often recommended to anchor the mind. This tool can be a sound, a word or a phrase. It can be neutral, that is one with no association, like the number one; a sound with a pleasant association, like mmm; something which evokes personal meaning, such as a reminder as in "pause," "focus," or "be present;" a significant message, like "It's not important;" or an affirmation like "I am free to be me."

While these can be used to help create a meditation state they can also be used as cues to monitor your awareness and regulate your mind when it starts to take off with a life of its own down memory lane, replaying the ever present old tapes. The one I like to keep me mindfully in the present when my mind starts to take off is "Return home."

Only in quiet waters things mirror themselves undistorted. Only in a quiet mind is adequate perception of the world.

—HANS MARGOLIUS

Guided Meditations

Guided meditations are used to actively or deliberately bring images into your awareness. The conscious creation of mental images and sensory experiences can serve as a tool to access your intuitive mind, allowing your logical mind to slip into the background. The following two meditations can be used to create a sense of inner peace and self-acceptance.

LETTING GO GUIDED MEDITATION

Lie on your back and gently close your eyes. Place your feet a comfortable distance apart and place your arms away from the sides of your body.

There's nothing you need to be doing right now. Let your mind become aware of the calm and serene flow of your breath. Consciously guide your breath so that it remains smooth and calm. Let go of all the tension in your body.

For the time being, let go of your worry, let go of your discouragement. Let all your apprehensions vanish. Trust that everything is all okay. Your life is unfolding just as it should. You are content to be who you are.

See yourself in a boat cast adrift on the sea, gently bobbing over the waves. You have put down your sail and your oars. You have stopped trying to row as hard as you can in one direction. You have given up the effort to force your boat in one direction by manipulating your situation and the people around you.

You have relinquished control—let go. Feel a calmness settle over you. You have turned your boat over to fate, recognizing that fortune never comes in the form you expect. You have given yourself over to the natural flow of the universe. You have let go.

Know that your boat is headed in a positive direction, and that—when the time is right—you will discover the lush shore toward which you are headed.

Accept that you don't have all the answers and that you don't know enough to be able to control everything. You can work with the forces in the universe that make things happen, but you don't have to make everything happen yourself.

Trust that things will work out wonderfully for you. Know that, no matter what happens, it will all work itself out for the best.

Let go of the struggle.

Let go of the panic.

Let go of the longing for things to be other than they are.

Feel your body floating and know that you have let go.

Feel a light, easy feeling come over you—a feeling of being free of a burden. Let this quiet settle over you like a cosmic tranquilizer. Experience a sense of inner peace and know that you are ready to accept life just as it unfolds.

Slowly bring yourself back to the present.

When you are ready, open your eyes.

▼

SELF-ACCEPTANCE GUIDED MEDITATION

Get comfortable. Close your eyes. Relax.

There is no place you need to be going right now. There's nothing you need to be doing. There's nothing to worry about.

Take a deep breath. As you breathe out, let go of all your tension. With each exhale, relax a little more. Feel yourself let go. Imagine you are standing beneath a warm shower of relaxation.

Relax your feet. Relax your lower legs. Relax your knees. Relax your thighs. Let your hips drop all tension. Feel your back completely relaxing. Let go of all tension in your stomach. Relax your chest. Relax your shoulders. Let your arms become completely limp and very heavy. Let go of all the tension in your neck. Let your head become very heavy. Relax all the muscles in your face. Relax your eyes, your cheeks, your jaw, your lips. Let go. Your whole body is very heavy, very relaxed.

Let a picture come into your mind of a very pleasant scene, any place in the world that you might go. It could be a place from your childhood. It could be the beach. It could be a mountain. It could be a meadow or a woods. Picture it in your mind's eye. Pretend that you are there. Bring it in clearly and vividly with all the senses. Hear the sounds around you there. Feel the feelings. See the colors and the movements around you. And most of all, let yourself feel the really good feeling of being in this most comfortable, relaxed place.

If any unnecessary thoughts come into your head, just let them float out again like clouds floating by, barely noticed.

As you continue to relax, let yourself recall a very pleasant experience, some time when you were feeling very good about yourself. You might have been active or quiet. It was a time when you felt really good—all over. There was a deep feeling that all's well. Perhaps you were with someone you really cared about. Maybe it was just a few days ago, maybe a month ago, or a year ago. Or maybe it was a time in your childhood. A time when you felt completely happy to be you. Let yourself go back there now. Whatever this time was, go back there now. Bring it in clearly.

Breathe easily, deeply.

Tune into that element of you that feels really good; the self-accepting element; the element of you that can say, "I accept myself. I accept myself fully and completely. I really feel good about who I am." You may find that these words repeat themselves in your head. "I accept myself. I feel good inside, all over. The good feelings I have about myself are totally unaffected by anyone else's opinions or judgments. I like myself. I'm glad I'm the person I am."

Let this feeling fill you completely. Let it fill every cell in your body.

Now, very slowly, begin to become aware of the room you are in. Keep this feeling of self-acceptance with you as you—very slowly—begin to move, first one foot, just a little bit, then one hand. As you move, keep this feeling. Slowly bring yourself back into the room, and after a while, open you eyes. Keep being aware of how you feel.

This feeling—this experience of self-acceptance—is always with you. You may lose track of it at times, but you can always find it again—whenever you wish. And the more you go to this place within, the more a part of your everyday life it will become.

You may lie here as long as you wish. There's no hurry to move.

▼

Mandates for Living Mindfully

When you live mindfully, you rely on your personal power. You have the moral courage to stand by your convictions. You don't let someone else's interpretation of how life works take the place of self-reflection and self-knowledge. You have no need to control others and you become impervious to outside influences of any kind.

The following five "mandates" are fundamental to living mindfully.

- Look within for answers

- Accept what is and give up the longing for things to be other than they are

- Feeling unloved is often a signal to be more loving, so when you feel unloved, be more loving

- You can control only your own actions, so don't try to control others

- Work to balance your actions with your beliefs

- **Look within for answers**

Insights into your own behavior and interactions are gained through continual self-reflection. You begin to rely more and more on self-evaluation as opposed to outside evaluation.

Learn to return to yourself.

—B. L.

⌒

As you become more in touch with your own "inner workings," in turn, this inner clarity about who you are and how you want to be allows you to become more sensitive to the needs of others. Paradoxically, the more you look within for answers the more you are able to see others' perspectives, recognize your own assumptions, and realize that what you view as reality is only *your* interpretation. Once you are able to consider the other person's perspective, you see that reality is often an alternate interpretation. The process of continually looking inside actually allows you to see others more clearly.

A critical factor in maintaining a positive frame of mind and healthy relationships is the capacity to examine your own actions and focus on your own choices rather than blaming another person, or hoping that person will change, or worse, trying to make the person change.

- **Accept what is and give up the longing for things to be other than they are**

When you long for things to be different than they are and focus your thoughts on what isn't rather than on what is, you are not fully in the present. Giving your attention to what might be rather than what is keeps you from finding the joy in what you have.

Desiring or preferring things to be other than they are is fundamentally different from longing. Longing is a kind of wishing that keeps you stuck with what is. If you merely long for something, you don't focus your energy toward allowing it to happen, instead you tend to build up resentment toward those who have what you want and you become envious. Resentment and envy are negative emotions and when your attention is given to negative thoughts, driven by a negative emotional state, you are disempowered to take personal action. Negativity depletes energy that could otherwise be directed toward engaging in positive change.

On the other hand, acceptance of what is and holding a basic belief that things will change for the better keeps you from sacrificing your present life for your future dreams.

Choose to fulfill your highest vision of yourself.

—B.L.

∽

• **Feeling unloved is often a signal to be more loving,
so when you feel unloved, be more loving**

When I feel unloved, this bad feeling sometimes can serve as a filter through which I "see" others' behavior. I use my ill feeling about myself as a lens through which I transform others' actions to conform with my projected interpretation of their behavior. This is classic projection.

It goes something like this: I feel unloved. I attribute my bad feeling to others' actions toward me. Because I feel unloved, I am resentful toward the person(s) who isn't meeting my needs. The resentment leads to my using negative behavior to retaliate for the hurt I'm feeling. Because I have attributed responsibility to another for causing my hurt I therefore blame that person. Now because it's someone else's fault, that person deserves to be punished.

Now here's what I have done. Not only have I relinquished responsibility for my own feelings but I have justified my punishing behavior. I'm using negative behavior to try to get positive behavior. I'm trying to control the behavior of others by losing control of my own behavior!

If instead I go "inside" rather than "outside" to look at my unloved feeling and pay attention to my own behavior I may discover that this bad feeling has permeated my thoughts and is causing me to act in unloving ways. What I really want is love and yet I am withholding love from those I want it from. Instead of relenting about others' behavior or trying to control others' behavior I can make the choice to change my own behavior and simply act more loving. Of course this is no guarantee that you will elicit more loving behavior but it's a far better shot than trying to coerce loving behavior with hurtful, blaming behavior.

- **You can control only your own actions,
  so don't try to control others**

We often try to control the behavior of others by dispensing rewards and punishments. In reality, we are able to control only our own behavior. The person on the receiving end still makes a choice. Now if we have authority over or higher status than the other person, that person may succumb to being controlled. However, in equal status relationships, trying to control others only leads to power struggles.

> *What is soft is strong.*
>
> —LAO TZU

Regarding intimate relationships, the only legitimate power or control we have in a relationship is to do one of two things—either make our own needs known, or change our own behavior to meet our partner's needs. More than that we can only ask for—we can't demand it, and we shouldn't expect it.

Attempting to control the other person's behavior ultimately only leads to conflict as that person attempts to meet his or her need for control. William Glasser in *Control Theory* considers the need for control to be one of the basic needs we all have. Whenever people feel that they do not have control they will do whatever they think is necessary to regain control.

The concept of control should be viewed as an inner action rather than a response to things and others around us, or an attempt to control others' behavior. Giving up trying to control others also frees us from the responsibility of their actions.

- **Work to balance your actions with your beliefs**

The key to self-fulfillment is to have your actions reflect your true beliefs. There is a whole generation of those of us who keep trying to get better, finally do it right by extending effort to be exposed to and learn the newest ways to get better. I am suggesting that we abandon this kind of effort. Instead we should work to clarify our basic beliefs and continually check out whether our actions are congruent with what we truly believe.

Until we achieve balance between what we do and what we believe there is still much to be done. But the "work" isn't merely learning a new skill, implementing a new technique or engaging in a new practice, rather it is a transformative process of continual examination and self-reflection for the purpose of aligning our values with our life's work and daily living. We need to perpetually ask ourselves "What is important to me?" and the follow-up question "Does what I'm doing fit with what I believe is important?". This is living the process of reflective practice.

> *... we need to learn to live as individuals in process.*
>
> —CARL ROGERS

Ten Basic Ideals to Endorse

When you endorse these ten ideals you can live in the here and now, accepting the gift of each day. You embrace life joyously and dare to live authentically and deliberately. You accept life's ironies and expand yourself, recognizing that you are part of a larger whole.

> *Nature goes her own way,*
> *and all that to us seems an exception*
> *is really according to order.*
>
> —GOETHE

- Question conventional wisdom

- Discover the joy in what you have

- Trust that things will work out as they should

- Have no expectations, only preferences

- Refrain from rating yourself

- Know the limits of your responsibility

- Accept ownership for your own feelings

- Treat others as equals

- Accept everyone

- Forgive and forget

• **Question conventional wisdom**

Conventional wisdom is nothing more than the collective societal mindset of how things ought to be. When you establish your own bounds you are not limited by the expectations of others. By challenging currently-held beliefs you expand your horizons and recognize that boundaries are arbitrary.

When you question conventional wisdom, creativity abounds and you can soar above the rest.

• **Discover the joy in what you have**

Delight in each day. Consider each day a new beginning. It's an opportunity for a fresh start. If yesterday was a bad day, erase the slate. Start each day with a clean slate. Make tomorrow a better day. With an attitude adjustment, you can resolve to begin anew.

> *Accept the gift of today by watching life with patience,*
> *acceptance and good humor.*
>
> —DIANE DREHER

Inject some warmth and recognition into someone's day. Don't pass up a chance to tell someone how he or she brought a smile to your face.

Be the bright spot in someone's day. Make positive assertions every day. Tell someone how you appreciate them.

Acknowledge others by expressing affection and appreciation. Tell a good friend: "Having a friend like you is really important to me."

- **Trust that things will work out as they should**

Preferring things to be different but accepting them as they are creates a state of mindfulness in which you trust that things will work out as they should. You don't give up the effort, you just give up the anxiety about reaching your goal. You trust that you are on the right path and accept life just at it unfolds. Continue your pursuit but leave behind the struggle. Endorse life with patient optimism.

> *You can't control outcomes but you can dare to pursue your desires.*
>
> —STEPHEN PAUL

- **Have no expectations, only preferences**

Holding unconditional expectations for yourself, others, or situations will keep you unfulfilled. Viewing life as awful when things do not go the way you would like them to go keeps you acting and feeling victimized. Having unreasonable expectations leads you to condemn yourself and others and to feel and act helpless. Unconditional expectations take the form of believing that things *must* or *should* be a certain way.

The healthier alternative is to prefer or desire things to be different but to work with the reality of the present situation. When things go wrong it's okay to be unhappy, frustrated, or angry but there is no need to become depressed and miserable. There is no need to make someone the victim.

Instead ask yourself "What can I do to change the situation?" and accept that sometimes the answer will be nothing. Then you need to ask of yourself "What do I need to do to make things more desirable?"

Eliminate absolute statements and replace shoulds, musts and oughts with wishes, desires and preferences.

- **Refrain from rating yourself**

Strive to eliminate all kinds of self-ratings. When you refrain from rating, evaluating or judging yourself you develop a protective shield to keep others' evaluations of you from penetrating.

Instead rate only your acts, deeds and performances. Rate acts as "good" when they are self-enhancing and "bad" when they are self-defeating. Becoming detached from your evaluation of your level of performance is the essence of self-acceptance. While you might prefer to be more capable, to have more, or to achieve more, accept your imperfections, mistakes, and vulnerabilities.

Don't try to prove yourself, strive to accept and enjoy yourself.

- **Know the limits of your responsibility**

You are responsible for your own feelings, not for others' feelings. Some people get hurt because they are unreasonably sensitive. Others use their hurt to manipulate you. Don' t try to protect people from themselves. There are natural consequences for every act. We often learn more from our mistakes than we do from our successes.

Openly and honestly expressing your feelings doesn't deny others' rights and needs. You can attribute responsibility to others without blaming.

Free yourself from the responsibility
of making others happy.

—STEPHEN PAUL

⌣

- **Accept ownership for your own feelings**

Your feelings are neither right nor wrong, they just are. You don't need to justify your feelings. So don't tell yourself you *shouldn't* feel the way you feel.

Don't deny your feelings. Don't blame others for the way you feel, they need to get their own needs met.

Be in touch with how you are feeling. Become aware of the words you use to express your feelings. Do you tend to say "I feel *like* ... (action) rather than just "I feel ... (feeling)?" Learn to give attention to what you're feeling. It helps to give your feeling a name.

- **Treat others as equals**

Treat everyone with respect. One person is as worthy as the next. Treating others as lesser beings is another form of judgment.

- **Accept everyone**

Accept others' right to choose,
      accept their choices,
            and accept their right to say no.

Allow yourself the same freedom.

Don't let others make choices for you.
      Refuse to allow others to judge your choices.
            Affirm that you too have the right to say no.

- **Forgive and forget**

When you let emotional attachment and investment in the past dissolve, you free yourself to move on. Letting the walls of resentment crumble melts the hardness in your heart allowing you to leave behind the resentment and move on with an open heart.

If we stay stuck in our resentment, we are diminished. Unforgiving behavior has natural consequences.

> *... the instrument of justice cuts both ways.*
> *Punishing others is punishing work.*
>
> —JOHN HEIDER

Ten Inclinations to Avoid

Avoiding these tendencies will help you stay in balance, focusing your attention inward rather than outward.

- Saying or thinking always or never

- Trying to prove yourself

- Denying your feelings

- Accepting responsibility for others' feelings

- Trying to control others

- Letting yourself be controlled by others

- Making choices for others

- Letting small irritations build into resentments

- Interpreting different as inferior

- Sacrificing your present life for your future dreams

Five Truths to Sanction

Constantly revisiting these principles helps you to stay centered and helps you to get back on course when you start to waver from your balance point.

- You have a great many more choices than you tend to recognize.

- You need to ask for what you want.

- It's what you tell yourself that makes you crazy.

- Your most important learnings will come from your most painful experiences.

- Change is a process, not an event; expect leaps and backslides.

Questions for Self-Inquiry

When you become your own counsel, self-questioning is an essential tool. Self-questioning can be the tool to create an opening of the heart and the mind.

Here are some questions to pose to go within for answers.

Questions for Self-Reflection

- What am I feeling?

- Is there something I am afraid of?

- Am I acting out of fear?

- Am I not acting out of fear?

- What is my hurt about?

- Is there something I need to say to someone?

- What message am I giving myself through my inner speech, or self-talk?

- What message is *my* behavior communicating?

- What assumptions am I making about another person's actions?

- Do I need to verify my assumptions?

- Am I trying to impose my beliefs and values on another person?

- Have I considered other possible interpretations of another person's behavior?

- What need might the other person be trying to meet?

- Did I ask for what I wanted?

- What can *I* do?

- What are my choices?

- Are there other choices I haven't acknowledged?

- How can I reposition the way I am seeing things?

- What am I doing? Is it getting me what I want? If not, what is it getting me?

- What am I doing that's not working?

Questions to Tap Your Inner Wisdom

Our inner wisdom knows the answer to our questions involving our being and becoming. Our deeper self speaks to us in symbolic fashion, through dreams, intuitive flashes, or perhaps a melody that runs through our minds for no seemingly apparent reason. Asking ourselves meaningful questions and being receptive to the answers that surface can inform our quest for self-knowledge. Try closing your eyes, ask the question and wait for an image or symbol to form in your mind. You may want to draw the image and then attempt to interpret its meaning. Or, you may want to try repeating the question several times before going to sleep to inspire your dreaming mind. Here are some possible questions to pose for your inner wisdom to ponder.

- What is keeping me from making a decision?

- What aspect of my life do I need to give attention to now?

- What is the next step in my personal transformation?

- What obstacles stand in the way of my taking the next step?

- What do I need to develop to overcome these obstacles?

Questions to Create a Felt Sense

Eugene Gendlin in *Focusing* suggests what he refers to as patient inner listening and tinkering to surface a *felt sense* when you are struggling with a problem. To help you go beneath the pain and hurt to a bodily sensing of something emerging, try the following series of questions when you are faced with a nagging problem.

- What's between me and feeling okay?

- What is in the way of feeling okay?

- What do I sense in my body when I think about the problem?

- What is the uneasiness, discomfort about?

- What is the essence?
  What's at the core of the issue?

- What is the worst of this feeling?

- Can I give it a name?
  Try this a number of times until you get the word that represents the felt sense.

- What am I really seeking?

- What would it feel like if it was okay?

Questions for Ongoing Self-Assessment

Here are some questions to pose to help you keep in mind that you have much control over what you do and the choices you make. You may want to make up a reaction sheet to record your answers on a regular basis to become more aware of your choices. After awhile, you can return to your sheets and try to identify any patterns you may be able to "nip in the bud." You can modify your list of questions to pay attention to based on your emerging awareness.

- Have I done something I really enjoy lately?

- Have I recently done something relating to something I care deeply about?

- What have I learned or relearned about myself?

- Do I have any unfinished business left over from last week (last month)?
  If so, how have I been carrying it around?

Chapter 10

Moving into Balance by Supporting Others

Supporting Others in Their Reflection and Inquiry

When you facilitate in the process of self-reflection you help others to experience that the answer is within. It's hard to help, not easy. Only healthy people can be good helpers, or Taoists nonhelpers.

> *The best path to be a good helper is to improve oneself;*
> *but the best way to improve oneself*
> *is to help others.*
>
> —ABRAHAM MASLOW

When you want to help others solve problems or deal with difficult situations, your job is to build trust in their own counsel, to reaffirm that the resolution is within. What you want to do is facilitate development of their own problem resolution, not provide a solution. You want to listen not only to their words, but also identify the underlying emotions and give voice to their feelings. In this process, it's important that they clarify their own assumptions and verify the accuracy of their assumptions.

When we respond with acceptance, we recognize and respond to the underlying feelings, conveying understanding and acceptance of those feelings. In doing so, we neither encourage nor discourage the feelings, we merely acknowledge them. Such acknowledgment helps others solve their own problems and keeps the responsibility with them.

What you really want is to be the mirror of reflection, so the picture become clearer—to help to unmuddy the waters. Perhaps to allow new alternatives to surface and to help them become aware that they don't have to accept other's judgment of their actions.

Here are some suggestions on what to do and what not to do.

1. Don'ts —When you want to help others self-reflect:

   • Don't give answers or provide solutions

   • Don't analyze or diagnose

   • Don't place blame or be judgmental

   • Don't ask why

*The degree to which I can create relationships
which facilitate the growth of others as separate persons
is a measure of the growth I have achieved
in myself.*

—CARL ROGERS

We frequently communicate with others by offering solutions and making judgments. Such messages communicate unacceptance and break down the interactive process. When we give solutions we send a message that we do not think the person is capable of coming up with his or her own solution. If the person gets this message, he or she could become resentful of the hidden message—you should do what I say.

Another common tactic is to try to "get to the heart of the matter," to push to get the other person to try to analyze what has happened. The typical vehicle is asking "why" questions. Why questions often impede the self-reflection process. Rather than promoting a helping relationship and building trust, asking "why" hints at criticism. The implicit assumption with the "why" question is that the person *should* have acted differently. This gives the message that you are judging not accepting the person.

For many, the word establishes a mindset of disapproval, e.g., "Why didn't you…?", "Why can't you…?", "Why are you…?", "Why do you have to…?" Thus feelings of being threatened or judged are often evoked, leading to either withdrawing or feeling the need to rationalize or defend themselves, distracting from the self-reflective process.

Although it is important for the person to come to an understanding of why he or she acted or reacted in a certain way, overtly asking why is less likely to get to the "real" why than an exploration directed by the person him or herself. Asking "why" doesn't leave a person free to explore or communicate what he or she sees as the issues. The why question tends to restrict the interaction and allows the helper to take over the direction of the interaction rather than enabling the owner of the problem to assume responsibility for solving the problem. In addition, when "why" questions are irrelevant and off-base, they can be very derailing. Since the helper is often on a "fishing expedition," many of the questions are off-target. Responding to these questions causes others to have to detour, diverting them from their own sense of the important issues. Asking "why" questions confines the person to the answer called for and severely limits the range of issues and feelings the person with the problem can address. The helper controls the discussion and literally programs the problem owner to depend on that person for resolution of the problem.

Asking *what, when, where,* and *how,* rather than *why* questions are more likely to help individuals gain insights that will help them clarify for themselves those factors which might be contributing to their problem situation. Listening and acknowledging feelings helps others understand their feelings and reflect on issues, leading to problem clarification and resolution.

2.   Dos —When you want to help others self-reflect:

- Listen with an open mind

- Communicate acceptance, not necessarily agreement

- Respect their feelings

- Be honest and self-disclose

- Acknowledge your assumptions

- Offer more than one interpretation

- Ask questions for reflection

Some examples of questions that aid self-reflection are:

- What would you lose by...?

- What would you gain by...?

- What would happen if...?

- Are there options you haven't considered?

- What assumptions are you making?

- Is there a way to reposition your interpretation of the situation?

We promote self-reflection when we provide encouragement rather than praise, respond with acceptance not judgment, and offer constructive interpretations rather than evaluative feedback or destructive criticism. We promote self-reflection when we encourage others to set their own standards, deal with their feelings and look within for the motives of their actions.

One of my dearest friends, seems always to say just the right thing to get me thinking about something I should be dealing with. By responding with acceptance, not with reprimands, and by posing questions which inspire self-reflection, she helps me to go inside and begin to look at what I am doing. Here are two examples.

As I was lamenting the characteristics which made my present partner the wrong choice, she pointed out that I seemed to know what I didn't want, but what about what I did want? It was a compelling thought. After that suggestion, I began to pay attention to what I was telling myself about the men in my life. When I did this, I realized I had set up an expectancy where I was just waiting for one of my disapproved traits to surface—one of my essential flaws, to be distinguished from mere nuisances. Oh, now his true colors are showing—he's a workaholic and I certainly don't want that. I thought he was proud of my successes, now I see he really resents my accomplishments and I won't have that! My actions were reactive rather than proactive. My expectancy was that it was just a matter of time before they failed the test—and they always did fail. My expectation served as a self-fulfilling prophesy.

Her asking me what I wanted helped me to reconcile making a choice for myself versus judging the other person. That is, I don't have to make the other person wrong or bad to make the right choice for myself. Right doesn't exist in any absolute sense, only as a preference.

On another occasion, I was saying I was in my current relationship because he needed a friend, he needed some support now, someone to listen without judgment, to be accepted for what he was and so on. The same friend commented "But what do you need?" By posing this question she helped me to go inside and begin to look at what my own needs were. She didn't offer advice, or try to console me, or judge my actions.

She didn't say you're always picking losers (and she might have had something there!), instead she honored my capacity to look at myself.

I think I had actually gotten through all of my relationships without ever asking that question. Of course, if I didn't ask *myself* what I needed, I also didn't explicitly ask for what I needed or wanted.

My pattern was to keep giving and giving until I became resentful that I wasn't getting. Once I was resentful, then all the traits I disliked seemed to appear. Then I could say he wasn't the right one anyway. It was all quite convenient.

When I read the dialogue of a couple Harville Hendrix wrote about it really seemed to hit home. He described a couple who were struggling with repressed anger. She described their life together by saying "It's really quite pleasant. We don't yell and we don't criticize each other (pause) at least not openly." Underneath this seemingly calm and considerate behavior was a sea of despair. Her spouse's commentary went like this: "I do something dumb, and she forgives me. I refuse to take responsibility for something, and she does it for me. We've got it all worked out: I'm difficult; she's wonderful. I hate it." They were locked into their roles, he as bad boy, she as the all-forgiving saint.

Her lack of anger allowed him to do anything he wanted to do and know that he wouldn't have to face her anger. It allowed him to be the irresponsible kid and know he wouldn't have to face any consequences. Her lack of expression of anger accommodated the unhealthy dynamic they had together. Staying in her saint role gave him permission to keep taking advantage. This was my realization, that my idea of being a together person meant that I didn't exhibit any inappropriate behaviors, I was all-forgiving, perfect! Waiting for my mate to prove himself unworthy.

Often our initial response to not getting our needs met is sadness. Sadness is a response that is sanctioned. A familiar message many of us grew up with is that it's okay to be sad, but not okay to be angry. Left to our own resources, our natural response typically is to let the sadness evolve into withdrawal and eventually, resentment.

Supporting Others in Their Pain

A very dear friend of mine was recently what she likes to call "physically challenged" with a life-threatening disease. She found that often others' attempts to be consoling were quite disconcerting. She said "I wanted to have my feelings acknowledged and validated. I didn't want my feelings to be ignored and I didn't want to be told what to feel, to think, or to do." In the process of attributing personal meaning to her challenge, she discovered that what others were calling the recovery process for her was not a recovery in the sense that you get over it, rather it was a sense of living with new realities—more of a *letting be* than a *letting go*.

Sometimes it takes a personal crisis for us to examine what we truly believe about life. Those who can move beyond the "Why me?" question and face the challenge with a spirit of living their lives to the fullest ask a very different question. They ask "What's preventing me from living my life as fully as I can?"

In *How to Survive the Loss of a Love*, the authors have this to say about pain: "Don't postpone, deny, cover or run from your pain. Be with it … The only way *out* is *through*."

When we want to support friends in pain we typically think we should do something. My experience is that it's the mere being there that our friends want.

> *Don't just do something, sit there!*
>
> —ROBERT FULGHUM

Parker Palmer in *The Active Life: Wisdom for Work, Creativity, and Caring* talks about how most of his friends tried to rescue him to no avail with well-intended advice when he was experiencing deep depression. One friend, however, took a different tack. Every afternoon around four o'clock he came, sat him in a chair, removed his shoes, and massaged his feet, hardly saying a word. But his presence provided a lifeline, a link to humanity.

It's hard to know what to say to a person who is wrestling with a personal crisis; it's easier to know what not to say. Anything which tries to minimize the person's pain (e.g., "It could be a lot worse."), or which asks the person to disguise or reject his or her feelings (e.g., "Don't take it so hard.") is likely to be unwelcomed.

Here are a few simple guidelines.

- Listen
  ...Just be there.

- Be quiet
  ...There's no need to fill the space with words.

- Don't try to distract or divert
  ...That only communicates "I'd rather not deal with this."

- Avoid advice in the form of "shoulds", "you better", "it's time to."
  ...They only foster guilt and a sense of inadequacy.

- Invite them to talk
  ...Offer an invitation, but accept their decline.

- Acknowledge their feelings
  ...Don't down-play the intensity of those feelings.

- Respect their needs
  ...Suppress the urge to impose what you think would be good for them.

- Honor their truth
  ...Accept that they know where they need to be with their pain.

Suspending Judgment

There is nothing either good or bad
but thinking makes it so.

—SHAKESPEARE

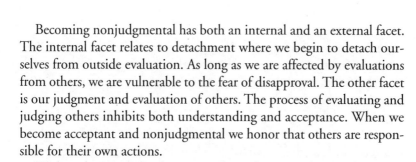

Becoming nonjudgmental has both an internal and an external facet. The internal facet relates to detachment where we begin to detach ourselves from outside evaluation. As long as we are affected by evaluations from others, we are vulnerable to the fear of disapproval. The other facet is our judgment and evaluation of others. The process of evaluating and judging others inhibits both understanding and acceptance. When we become acceptant and nonjudgmental we honor that others are responsible for their own actions.

We have been socialized to respond to others in judgmental ways, so most of our responses to others are judgmental. We judge a behavior to be positive or negative and respond accordingly in judgmental language—that's good or that's bad. When we evaluate the behavior of another, even with a positive evaluation, we are trying to exercise control over that person. If we say "that's superior," we are implicitly reserving the right to also say "that's inferior." Positive evaluations in the form of praise promote the idea that the value of what one does is determined by the way others evaluate its worth.

So when I say "you're right" I'm really saying that's what I believe and what I believe is right. Incidentally, if I say "you're wrong" I'm saying not agreeing with me is wrong as if I set the standards by which others should act. Or when I say "that's an excellent point" I'm really saying you're interpretation is in agreement with mine and therefore I judge it to be good. Praise encourages others to seek outside evaluations for their accomplishments and perpetuates an attitude of conformity to external standards. Also, evaluation, even in the form of praise, puts one in a position of judgment, signifying a higher status level.

Praise is positive evaluation of others, whereas encouragement is acceptance and support. Encouragement consists of words or actions that con-
vey respect and belief in the capabilities of others. Encouragement
demonstrates acceptance and stimulates motivation from within allowing others to become aware of their own strengths. When we give encouragement we help others accept their imperfections; when we give praise
we train others to fear disapproval. Although it is often assumed that
being judgmental means being judgmental negative, being judgmental is
also being judgmental positive. Evaluating the actions of others as good
or right, or responding with a positive judgment is still judgment.

In the classroom setting, children are often conditioned to equate their
worth with whether or not they know the right answer. Teachers frequently attribute qualities of a student's work to the student's personality
(i.e., "you're lazy" when students don't finish their work, "you didn't
try" when students get the wrong answer). When teachers use praise to
tell students they are good because they know the right answer, students
logically conclude that they are bad when they do not know the answer.
This entrenched practice of equating knowing the "right" answer with
goodness is dangerous and has far-reaching impact on the child's development of a sense of self-worth.

Often teacher-student patterns of communication are dehumaniz-
ing rather than humanizing. Teachers typically are not sensitive to the
pervasive power of the messages students internalize. They often fail
to recognize that the messages they communicate to students have a
cumulative effect and can serve to erode their self-esteem. Children who
don't do well in school typically have low estimations of their self-
worth. This can lead to involvement in gangs and rebellious acts to
try to rebuild their low self-esteem and get the positive recognition they
never got in the classroom.

In pursuing my shift from judgmental ways of responding to others to
acceptant ways of responding to others, my family, friends and colleagues
would frequently become frustrated and press for evaluations of their
actions. They often persisted with questions like "Do you think I did the
right thing?" On the other hand, those who endorsed the effort and sanctioned my reasoning for making the shift would often ask "If I don't react

with a judgmental positive or a judgmental negative response, how *do* I respond?"

Learning to respond in nonjudgmental ways involves changing behavior which is well-ingrained. Some of us may initially need to use active practice techniques (i.e., specific prompting or cueing strategies, or overtly practicing new ways of acting and reacting) to replace judgmental responses with nonjudgmental responses. For some, self-reflection in the form of self-questioning will be all that it will take to curtail judgmental responses. For those whose judgmental behavior is more entrenched, I offer a beginning.

My general recommendations are to demonstrate acceptance and recognize efforts while conveying respect for the ability of others to solve their own problems and make the choices that are the appropriate choices for them. Give feedback from the heart rather than the head, by giving appreciative rather than evaluative feedback. Evaluative feedback is characterized by judgment (I am the judge, you are the judged) and typically takes the form of "you are…," "you are a…,? or "your…is…" On the other hand, appreciative feedback is more personal and focuses on letting others know how you have been affected by what they have done, either positively or negatively. When you come from the heart, you make a personal connection.

Here are some ways to respond that are nonjudgmental.

1. Give personal reactions without value judgments.

   - I like how you tell a story to make your point.

   - I enjoy your humor.

2. Describe your own feelings.

   - I was moved by the way you were able
     to comfort Joan.

   - I appreciate the way you were able to express
     your feelings. It makes me feel closer to you.

3. Provide honest recognition.

- It must be hard to accept that.

- I know this is a difficult time for you.

- I sometimes have the same fears.

4. Pose questions which expand the person's thinking.

- Can you identify what you are afraid of?

- Have you considered other possible interpretations of what he did?

Communicating in Nonblameful Ways

Meaningful communication often breaks down because one or both parties continually tells the other what's wrong with him or her. These messages serve to block further productive communication and move it to confrontation, a battle of attack and counterattack, creating an adversarial climate rather than a spirit of cooperation. Such messages inhibit and sometimes completely stop the two-way process of communication that is vital to maintaining relationships.

The goal of any relationship is the mutual meeting of wants and needs. Expressing dissatisfaction can be done either in a way that is facilitative, or in a way that is obstructive, making it more difficult to maintain an amicable relationship. Making others aware of the consequences of their actions without trying to make them feel guilty or ashamed tends to get two people in a cooperative frame of mind rather than a competitive one. Such messages are undistorted by assumptions about the other person. You can attribute responsibility to others without blaming them by communicating your feelings about how their actions affect you. Feelings are what they are; they should not be evaluated in terms of right or wrong, good or bad.

As an example, suppose you are frustrated because your son John is interrupting you while you're trying to talk on the phone. His interrupting is causing you a problem—you are feeling frustrated. If your message to John is "John, you're being rude," you are in effect blaming John for having whatever need prompted him to interrupt you. In doing so you avoid responsibility for your own feeling of frustration. If you had sent a message that accurately portrayed what was going on inside you, it would inevitably have been in "I" language, not in "you" language, as in "I'm frustrated because I can't talk and listen at the same time." While this message communicates what you are experiencing, the first message is a negative judgment about John. From John's perspective, he hears an evaluation of how bad he is in the first case, and a statement of fact about you in the second case.

Using I language puts responsibility for what is happening where it belongs, inside the person experiencing the problem. When you send messages about how you are affected and consequently feel, you take responsibility for your own inner condition and you leave the responsibility for the other person's actions with that person. Stating the consequences of the actions of others is valuable for two reasons. First, it helps you understand more clearly why you were bothered or pleased by what the person did. And secondly, telling others about the consequences of their actions can clarify for them the results of their actions. As with interpretations, we often think others *should* be aware of consequences without being told; but the fact is, they often aren't. By explicitly stating consequences, you can be sure that you leave nothing to their imagination.

Nonblameful messages don't require justification from the other person because they don't imply a negative evaluation. When there is no accusation of wrongful behavior, there is no need to become defensive, self-worth is not at stake. Sending I-messages instead of you-messages helps maintain a positive relationship by promoting consideration by others of the impact of their actions and fosters a willingness to change. Also, when you focus on sending a message from within it can sometimes help you recognize when your feelings are resulting from trying to impose your values and/or expectations on others rather than stemming from a violation of your own rights and feelings.

When you let others know exactly what's causing the problem with a nonblameful description of the situation and address the concrete effect on you, it communicates why the behavior is causing a problem for you.

It is a factual account without "editorial commentary." When evaluation creeps in you get messages that may sound nonblameful but are actually blameful messages in disguise as in "When I find I can't trust you..." (i.e., you're not trustworthy).

Often when we attempt to communicate our true feelings, we actually express not our feelings but our interpretations or intentions. For example, if you say "I feel like leaving." you have expressed an intention not a feeling. In this case, the feeling behind this statement is most likely hurt or anger. Or, we may disguise a feeling behind a message that's an interpretation such as saying "I feel you're wrong." This phrase doesn't express any feeling; it is merely our interpretation. Another example of a disguised you-message is: "When you stay out late with your friends I feel you are being inconsiderate." "I feel" is substituted for "I think" transforming the message from a true feeling message to a blaming, judgmental "you're inconsiderate" message. A feeling message would be "When you stayed out late, I got worried that something had happened to you."

When you avoid blame-attributing messages, you keep the focus on the impact of the behavior rather than on the person's shortcomings. When you get upset at others, what usually happens is that their actions create an effect on you and it is this consequence that generates the feeling. When you send the message that the feeling is being attributed to the actual or possible effect, not directly on the person's action, then the message is nonblameful.

Being blamed often elicits scary feelings held over from childhood. "You are bad" statements call up these old scary feelings and our old defenses against them. In childhood, being told by your parents "you're bad" caused feelings of worthlessness; being told by your parents you did something bad often led to punishment. Being criticized, belittled and punished led to negative emotional feelings causing counter-aggressive behavior and often a desire for revenge or retaliation. As an adult, hearing these kinds of messages still elicits defensive reactions, typically taking the form of a counter put-down or accusation.

Making "should" statements has a similar effect. Saying to others "You should do this" or "You should have done this" makes you their voice of conscience. The typical response to such moralization or implied or expressed criticism is for the person to attempt to prove that what he or she did was right, as in the statement "I wasn't disrespectful to your mother, I was just telling the truth." Often they take it one step further by trying to justify the behavior under the circumstances. Having to defend oneself is often accompanied by a counterattack in retaliation for your character assault, either implicitly or explicitly making you just as bad, or even worse, as in the following example. "I have a right to talk however I want to your mother. Why should I talk nicer to your mother? She never says anything nice to me, or anyone else for that matter. That's probably why you turned out the way you did." The battle lines are drawn as each tries to be right and make the other person wrong.

When you send a message that depicts your own feeling, you are exposing yourself as you really are, revealing your own vulnerability for being hurt or upset. Being able to identify your feelings is crucial because your feelings can radically affect both your interpretations as well as the messages you send. Feelings are often difficult to express, and we aren't always aware of our feelings. Also, expressing our feelings can carry the risk of an adverse reaction. Being able to identify how we feel can help to communicate more openly and honestly.

PERSONAL EXERCISE

Becoming Aware of Blameful Messages

We often explicitly (or implicitly) blame others for our feelings rather than reveal our own vulnerability for being hurt or upset. To become more aware of the messages you send, try taking time to reflect on the language you use to confront others with their actions that effect you.

The next time you find yourself confronting someone about a behavior that was upsetting to you, be aware of how you sent your message.

Questions for Self-reflection:

• Was there a direct or implied message of blame?

• Did I describe rather than label the person's behavior?

• Did I clarify the consequence the behavior had on me?

• Did I take responsibility for my own feeling?

• Did I express how I was feeling?

Developing the Art of Listening

Brenda Ueland in the late '50s, long before the merits of being a good listener were touted, wrote about "...the great and powerful thing that listening is," contrasting "good" listening with "no-good" listening, the kind that is ungenerous—critical, passive, censorious. She noted that the same principle of having your jokes laughed at applies to being listened to. If a person laughs at your jokes you become funnier and funnier, but if not, every little joke inside you "weazens up and dies." In the same vein, when you are listened to it helps you unfold and expand.

... listening, not talking, is the gifted
and great role,...

—BRENDA UELAND

Listening is a creative force. When someone listens to us with quiet attention and with silent affection, our creative fountain begins to bubble over. When you pour out your problems to a good listener then somehow you discover what to do about it yourself. A good listener lets you be recklessly yourself, at your worst, letting you show your soul. A good listener creates a nurturing climate, becoming the mirror of self-reflection, allowing the emergence of self-knowledge.

If you are a good listener, people want to be in your radius. A good listener has a kind of magnetic force drawing people in and around. The benefits of being a good listener are mutual. An alternating current is created which recharges both the listener and the person speaking so both are constantly recreated and neither gets tired of the other. They are connected on a deeper level and the insights of the person speaking spark insights for the listener as well.

When you are able to really listen, you hear not only what people are saying but what they are trying to say, you sense their real existence.

*The reality of the other person is not
in what he reveals to you. Therefore, if you would
understand him, listen not to what he says but rather to
what he does not say.*

—KAHLIL GIBRAN

Listening is perhaps the most overlooked form of communication, and probably the most essential element of any supportive relationship. Listening is the essence of comforting, nurturing and supporting others.

Often we get caught up in a "your turn/my turn" response format in which each person is only waiting for the other to stop talking so he or she can have his or her own turn to talk. This is the kind of nonlistening we typically encounter at cocktail parties, characterized by fragmented conversation in which neither person really listens to or cares what the other person has said. Probably the most exasperating nonlistening is when the person appears to be listening but responds with a comment completely unrelated to what you said. That's when you want to scream "You didn't hear a word I said!" Nonlistening can be extremely frustrating because the person is hearing the words but *not* listening to the message, often preoccupied with his or her own thoughts. These ways of interacting masquerade as listening but are poor substitutions for the real thing, exemplifying "no-good" listening.

Developing the art of listening helps you support others in the process of learning to go inside and trust their own counsel. Merely listening is an effective tool because it invites the person who may be experiencing a problem to talk about what is bothering him or her. Just being there, in silence, communicates caring. Remaining a silent listener allows others to release thoughts and feelings. So the first tool for developing the art of listening is *silence.* For many, it's difficult to just listen. Our tendency is to want to jump in with our own problems and solutions to the person's problem.

If you catch yourself trying to move in with a solution, try counting from 1 to 10 to yourself. You can learn to listen by staying in the present, perhaps saying to yourself something like "Be aware of what is happening now. My friend is talking. I am listening. I am quiet. I hear every word. I have endless time."

While silence communicates some degree of caring by just being there, it doesn't necessarily communicate acceptance. So the second tool in developing the art of listening is to demonstrate acceptance. You show acceptance by letting the person know you are really present by providing nonverbal and verbal support. Nodding or leaning forward show that you are *tuned-in*; minimal verbal responses such as "Uh-huh" or "Oh" offer encouragement to continue and serve to reassure the person that you are still attentive and interested.

Being silent and demonstrating that you are truly present communicate caring and acceptance, but they don't necessarily communicate that you are willing to take the time to help them delve into and explore their issues and concerns. So we need to move to the next tool in developing the art of listening which is to explicitly provide an invitation to talk. This involves a more proactive role on the part of the listener to ask open-ended, nonevaluative questions that invite the person to talk more. The listener might ask "Do you want to tell me about what happened?" or "Can you say more about what that felt like?" These kinds of "door-openers" serve as genuine invitations to share feelings or concerns. They let the person know that you want to help and that you are willing to take the time. But in order to keep the door open it's important to demonstrate understanding as well so the person talking knows you're understanding what's going on with him or her. This is why we need to move to the next tool in the art of listening, "active listening."

In active listening we become an interactive partner with the person, serving as the person's "mirror of understanding." This tool involves greater interaction and provides ongoing feedback, or *proof*, that you understand. The active listener "listens" for the underlying emotions as well as the words. As an active listener, you facilitate the person's development of his or her own problem resolution, you do *not* provide a solution. You also facilitate self-reflection. When you are serving as an active listener your role is merely to reflect, paraphrase and clarify what you are hearing. When you reflect you verbalize the feelings and attitudes that you perceive lie behind the message. Because spoken words often don't clearly articulate how one is feeling, responding in terms of the person's perspective, not your own, by feeding back the feelings perceived can help bring a troublesome emotion to the surface. In many cases, going beyond the spoken word to the often unspoken emotions can actually help the person identify his or her feelings, and assume ownership for them.

When you paraphrase you restate what you got as the basic message in as few words as possible. You translate and feedback to the person the essence of the basic message, in a simpler, more concise manner. When you paraphrase, you demonstrate understanding of what was said *without* adding any new ideas, or trying to analyze. The following is an example of paraphrasing. "In other words, the issue of cleaning up the house is not as important to you as whether I care about you, and when I didn't help you, you took it as a sign I didn't care." As illustrated in this example, paraphrasing makes one's assumptions explicit. While the simple step of restating what you thought you heard and playing it back to the person might seem unnecessary, it often helps the person take a more objective look at what he or she is saying.

Sometimes there is a need to sort out a statement you are confused about. Then you need to check out what you think you are hearing to clear up any confusion you might be having in understanding the message. Clarifying involves restating what the person said, stating your own confusion and asking for help or clarification (e.g., "I'm not sure how you feel. Earlier you said you were disappointed, now you seem to be saying something different. I'm confused." or "Let me see now, in other words it made you really happy, but you feel guilty about it making you happy? Is that it?").

Listening to Enhance Communication

These tools for listening can be used not only when you're trying to support another person who has a problem, they are also effective to enhance communication. They can be used in a more proactive way to keep the lines of communication open, especially between intimate partners.

Listening in a proactive way can facilitate communicating and resolving conflicts. To accurately reflect and paraphrase your partner's message, you have to really listen, rather than rehearsing in your mind the next thing you are going to say as you wait for your partner to finish talking.

If you haven't listened, you get to learn about it when your partner gives a resounding "no" to your reflection or paraphrase. Then you get to try again, listening more intently this time. Not only are you more likely to get your partner's message, your partner feels better about the communication process knowing he or she has been heard.

Reflecting, paraphrasing and clarifying as communication tools serve the important function of minimizing semantic differences. When you reflect back to your partner how you think he or she feels it helps you to stay in tune with your partner's feelings. It also helps you refrain from blaming, criticizing, or attacking. When you reflect you acknowledge and accept. When you merely feed back your partner's feelings it keeps you from becoming defensive and taking on responsibility for his or her feelings. When you reflect you are honoring your partner's feelings rather than evaluating or denying those feelings. When you become accustomed to hearing an issue with concern for the other person, you don't hear it as a criticism and have a need to defend, take responsibility for, or counterattack.

A reflection spoken in a calm, accepting tone of voice gives two messages: "I hear you saying this" and also "It's okay to be thinking or feeling these things. These are not horrible, though they might be disconcerting, and we can deal with them." Hearing a very scary aspect of yourself reflected in an unafraid manner helps you become more accepting of yourself and your fears.

Often the way we communicate merges our sensory input with our inferences or interpretations based on what we've seen, heard, or felt. An interpretation is a more abstract thought adding meaning to what we observed. Problems often arise when we treat our interpretations as if they were fact. It's important to stay aware of the difference between what actually happens and your interpretation of what happened. Interpretation is the process of attaching meaning to actions or situations; interpretations are *subjective*. That is, there is more than one interpretation that we can attach to any action or situation. Most of us resent others jumping to conclusions about the reasons for our actions. Learning to check out our perceptions and interpretations can serve as a reminder that what we see as reality is filtered through our own interpreting mind. The idea is to change your mindset by getting in the habit of entertaining other plausible alternative explanations for the actions of others.

One way to begin to see other interpretations is to actually offer more than one interpretation, by describing the other person's action, and posing two possible, different interpretations, and requesting feedback. If I can see only my interpretation, I make assumptions about the other person's behavior and act on that assumption; by entertaining, and actually stating, another interpretation, I can open up to seeing the other person's perspective as well.

Interpretations are based on more than simple sense data. They grow out of many factors, including past experience, assumptions, expectations, knowledge, attitude, and feelings.

- *Your past experience*

    What you have experienced yourself as well
    as what you have witnessed in the behavior
    of others influences your interpretation.
    (When I'm preoccupied with personal problems
    I draw away from my friends.)

- *Your assumptions*

    Based on your values and belief system, you
    make assumptions about the behavior of others.
    (An unkept promise is a sign of uncaring.)

- *Your expectations*

    You set up expectations by projecting your
    thoughts and what you would do in a particular
    situation. (I would never do that to anyone.)

- *Your knowledge*

    The information and skills available to you
    affect the inferences you make about the behavior
    of others. (Long-time, habitual cigarette smokers
    aren't even aware of lighting up.)

- *Your current mood*

> Your current frame of mind and attitude affect
> your interpretation. Your feelings, perceptions
> of self, and outside influences can all have an
> effect on how you attribute meaning to what is
> happening. (I feel good about life in general so
> I'm just not going to worry about what he says.)

There's nothing wrong with making interpretations. In fact, this is a necessary step because only by interpreting behavior do we arrive at meaning. However, we often make inaccurate interpretations, and when we don't separate actions from our interpretations of those actions, we can sometimes fool ourselves into believing that our interpretations are reality—that is, what we *think* is what *is*.

People give different interpretations to the same actions. Even if they agree on the actions, they may disagree on their inferences based on the actions, leading to miscommunication. Communicating based on your inferences rather than your observations can lead to misunderstandings and to disagreements, sometimes leaving the other person without a clue as to what happened. Often our interpretations are inaccurate, and when we don't separate actions from our personal interpretations, we treat our interpretations as reality.

It can also be helpful to learn to express your interpretation as such rather than presenting it as *fact*. Consider the difference between saying "If you cared about me, you wouldn't be late." and "When you were late, I thought you didn't care about me." Your comments are much less likely to put the other person on the defensive when you present them as the way you interpreted what happened rather than fact.

Building a Spirit of Community and Cultivating Friendships

Having a sense of community with others is an essential ingredient of self-fulfillment. Community is a state of mind; it's a feeling of connectedness to a larger whole. When you see yourself as a member of a world community, you see each person in this world community as just another soul searching for the meaning of its existence, pondering the great questions of life.

Fritjof Capra tells us that the principles of sustainable communities of plants and animals in nature are the very same principles that sustain human communities. These basic principles of ecology are the principles of interdependence, partnership, and diversity. We operate in many realms and spheres. We participate in life at multiple levels, within multiple communities, and partake in multiple roles. We interact with ourselves, friends, family members, and coworkers. We are citizens of our neighborhood, community, city, nation, planet, and universe. These principles of sustainable communities are now being explored in classrooms, in boardrooms, in living rooms, indeed at every level in which we come together in a spirit of community, a collective concern for humankind.

New terms such as ecopsychology and deep democracy embody these principles. Arnold Mindell defines deep democracy as a belief in the inherent importance of all parts of ourselves and all viewpoints in the world around us. Deep democracy is an attitude that the world is here to help us become whole, and that we are here to help the world become whole. It represents our sense of responsibility to follow the flow of nature and energy. Proponents of ecopsychology are redefining mental health to include a harmonious, respectful relationship with nature. Similarly, as we redefine personal growth as self-transformation, we extend the concept of health and well-being beyond the self-absorbed personal boundaries of the past two decades to include the health of our community and our world, and the well-being of our neighbors, both local and global.

Scott Peck defined community as a group of people who have learned to communicate honestly with each other, whose relationships go deeper than their masks of composure, and who have developed a commitment to rejoice together, to delight in each other and to make others' conditions their own. The principles of open and honest communication, mutual vulnerability, and collective responsibility for the human condition are at the heart of community-building.

The existence of community encompasses three Cs—commonality, caring, and connectedness. A sense of common bond defines our commonality; a sense of belonging and self-identity defines our connectedness. Concern for the welfare of the members of the community, open communication and honest interactions define a caring community.

Embracing a spirit of community is different from being a member of a defined community. A structured community could take the form of a support group, as in a single parent group or a couples workshop. We do find comfort in being and sharing experiences with those with similar plights. Or, it could take the form of a political or social organization where we join together with like-minded people with shared values. Or we may form a study group to get together with people with like interests or similar intellectual pursuits, as in a book club. Or we may form a group with others with similar expertise so we can pool our experience and knowledge, trusting that a collective viewpoint is better than a singular one. I have recently formed a working study group with colleagues who are doing qualitative research. We meet on a monthly basis as a task group to bring our problems, concerns and issues to the group, not only for recommendations and advice but for emotional support and comfort. In all of these types of communities we come together for a common purpose, for the "communal good" of the group, as well as to meet our individual needs for affiliation and acceptance.

The kind of community I am referring to adds another dimension. While there is a sense of working together, we maintain our individuality. We do not lose our own identity for the common good. We find solace in connecting on a deeper level but we don't have to give up any part of our true self. What we give is our attention and our affection.

We give generously of our time and we also ask for help when we need it. We look for opportunities in our interactions with others to grow in wisdom and in love. We bask in the sheer pleasure of an other's company. My greatest moments of intimacy have come not during love-making but in being on the listening end as someone chooses me to entrust their deepest fears. When I have opened my heart to a friend, I am most in touch with myself.

As a prerequisite to cultivating friendships, you must first become a compassionate friend to yourself. Learn to notice your internal conversations and begin to cultivate an inner friend who can dispel your fears and temper your self-criticism. Learn to become a trusting, accepting guardian to yourself. A sense of community is created from within. If you build your inner community, then it will extend outward. Acting in a spirit of community changes not only the community but the person as well.

Surround yourself with caring relationships. Deepen you bonds with friends, family members, co-workers, neighbors. Celebrate birthdays and nolidays, create special events, develop rituals. Put friendship above all else. In true friendships you can be recklessly yourself, you can be angry, nasty and cantankerous (at least once in a while!). You can expose yourself as you really are. True friendships can withstand the weird and the painful. Friendships create electricity, continually recharging and regenerating, connecting friends on a deeper level.

I have found as I continue to work on becoming nonjudgmental, more and more people want to confide their secrets to me. I know the deepest and darkest secrets of some people I hardly know. When you are nonjudgmental, you refrain from evaluating things as good or bad and accept people the way they are. You don't expect them to act the way you would act. By shedding the burden of judgment, we open up to others. When we offer encouragement it conveys our respect and belief in others' capabilities. When we demonstrate acceptance it stimulates motivation from within allowing others to become aware of their own strengths and accept their imperfections.

Unlike family ties where there is an unwritten claim on each other to live in certain ways, friendships don't require conformity or even compatibility. Because there are no issues of power and control, friend-ships foster acceptance. Deepening your bonds with family members will require moving out of your expected and familiar family roles. With family, friends and co-workers, we adopt roles that define and confine our interactions and serve to limit the feelings and thoughts we experience, as well as our understanding of ourselves and others. In order to change our roles we have to be willing to surrender a known way of defining ourselves for one that is unknown. Our familiar roles are accepted and reinforced by others; a change in role is likely to be unsupported by others who have come to expect us to fulfill certain roles. As with victim and rescuer, roles exist in mutually-reinforcing sys-tems. When one starts to change, the others become threatened and the system is thrown into crisis, thereby increasing the pressure not to change. However, even a small change can break open the system and create an opening for greater possibilities.

Challenging Confining Roles

This exercise can help you become more aware of your limited perceptions and help you to break through barriers of assumed roles.

1. On a sheet of paper make three columns.

2. In the first column...
   list all the things another person does that bothers you.

3. In the second column...
   write the name of the person in your family who did that.

4. In the third column...
   write something positive about it.
   (Example: If the bothersome behavior is never finishing anything, the positive aspect could be that the person is not compulsive.)

Questions for Self-reflection:

To challenge the roles that confine your interactions ask yourself:

- What roles do I play for others?

- What keeps me in these roles?

- Are these roles really helpful to others, or do they serve to confine others to their roles?

- What role do others adopt in response?

- What is the cost of staying in role?

- What feelings have been given up?

As we tried to strengthen our family ties, we set about trying to convert our sibling relationships to lifelong friendships. As part of this process, I had to get in touch with the multiple roles I was playing. First, and foremost of all my roles, was the role of the peace maker. I found myself always trying to patch things up and trying to keep the ship sailing smoothly. This role often caused bad feelings with my siblings because they viewed me as not being real and not dealing with my feelings. I had reciprocal negative feelings toward my sisters and brother because I put expectations on them to also keep peace. In addition to my general role, I had a role I played with each of my siblings. With my older sister, I was the compliant younger sister, playing into her need to be right. With my middle sister, I accepted her defining of my role as compensator for her feelings of being unloved as a child. There was this unspoken family dynamic that we treaded softly with her because she was so sensitive. This played out for me as my always having to be the one to call, or write, or invite. I was always the initiator. With my brother, I was the rescuer. When he was in trouble he would always call. When he needed money I would always lend it. I was the helper, he was the needy. With my "baby" sister, I was the counselor and the problem-solver.

When I finally realized how confining these defined roles were, I was able to see how each of these roles inhibited intimacy. The route to becoming friends was to first acknowledge our mutual roles, and then to accept that these roles kept us from being real friends and developing intimacy. We each committed ourselves to seeking out the answers to the question of what it would take to become lifelong friends. So for me it meant challenging my "big" sister on her need to be right by standing firm on my own convictions about nonjudgment. With my middle sister, it was requesting reciprocity and setting limits for how far I was willing to go to maintain our relationship. With my brother, it was making it clear what I expected from a friend and asking for what I needed from him. With my youngest sister, it was to abandon my enabler role, to stop trying to help by solving her problems for her.

Braking through the barriers of our assumed roles helped us to break through the walls of resentment, allowing us to become real friends and develop intimacy with each other. This process involved recognizing, accepting and challenging the roles that we let define and confine our relationships. These roles carry with them the excess baggage of expectations and their implicit judgments. Friendship requires acceptance, and acceptance is the opposite of judgment. Only when the fear of judgment is taken away can true friendship unfold.

Epilogue

The key to fulfillment is for each of us to penetrate the meaning of our existence. This is the voyage of expanding awareness through which our true self unfolds. The more we explore, the more we discover. The more we question, the more we open up to new realms of possibility. Moving into balance is the right of passage to bringing harmony into our lives. It is the journey where we find our personal balance between a constant struggle and the flow of awareness.

References

Bernard, M. E. 1986. *Staying Rational in an Irrational World.* New York: Carol Publishing Group.

Borysenko, J. 1987. *Minding the Body, Mending the Mind.* New York: Bantam Books.

Capra, F. 1983. *The Turning Point: Science, Society, and the Rising Culture.* New York: Bantam Books.

Chopra, D. 1993. *Creating Affluence.* San Rafael, CA: New World Library.

Cloke, K. 1990. *Mediation: Revenge and the Magic of Forgiveness.* Santa Monica: Center for Dispute Resolution.

Colgrove, M., Bloomfield, H. H., & McWilliams, P. 1991. *How to Survive the Loss of a Love.* Los Angeles: Prelude Press.

Covey, S. 1990. *The Seven Habits of Highly Effective People.* New York: Simon & Schuster.

Crum, T. F. 1987. *The Magic of Conflict: Turning a Life of Work into a Work of Art.* New York: Simon & Schuster.

Csikszentmihalyi, M. 1993. *The Evolving Self: A Psychology for the Third Millennium.* New York: HarperCollins.

Dreher, D. 1990. *The Tao of Inner Peace* . New York: HarperPerennial.

Dryden, W., & DiGiuseppe, R. 1990. *A Primer on Rational-Emotive Therapy.* Champaign, IL: Research Press.

Edelman, J., & Crain, M. B. 1993. *The Tao of Negotiation.* New York: HarperBusiness.

Ellis, A., & Harper, R. A. 1975. *A New Guide to Rational Living.* North Hollywood: Wilshire Book Company.

Epstein, S. 1993. *You're Smarter Than You Think.* New York: Simon & Schuster.

Fagan, J., & Shepherd, I. L. 1971. *Gestalt Therapy Now.* New York: Harper & Row.

Fulghum, R. 1988. *All I Really Need To Know I Learned in Kindergarten.* New York: Ivy Books.

Gendlin, E. T. 1981. *Focusing.* New York: Bantam Books.

Glasser, W. 1984. *Control Theory.* New York: Harper & Row.

Gottman, J. 1994. *Two-Part Harmony: Why Marriages Succeed or Fail.* New York: Simon & Schuster.

Harvey, J. R. 1988. "The Mind and Stress." *The Quiet Mind,* ed. by J. Harvey, 85-132. Honesdale, PA: The Himalayan International Institute.

Heider, J. 1985. *The Tao of Leadership.* New York: Bantam Books.

Hendrix, H. 1988. *Getting the Love You Want.* New York: HarperCollins.

Kabat-Zinn, J. 1994. *Wherever You Go, There You Are: Mindfulness Meditation in Everyday Life.* New York: Hyperion.

Kobasa, S. C. 1979. "Stressful Life Events, Personality, and Health: An Inquiry into Hardiness." *Journal of Personality and Social Psychology*, 37(1).1-11.

Kornfield, J. 1993. *A Path with Heart*. New York: Bantam Books.

Kramer, P. 1993. *Listening to Prozac*. New York: Viking Penguin.

Mindell, A. 1992. *The Leader as Martial Artist* . San Francisco: HarperSanFrancisco.

Moore, T. 1994. *Soul Mates: Honoring the Mysteries of Love and Relationship*. New York: HarperCollins.

Nelson, P. 1993. *There's a Hole in My Sidewalk*. Hillsboro, OR: Beyond Words Publishing.

Page, S. 1990. *If I'm so Wonderful, Why am I Still Single?* New York: Viking Penguin.

Page, S. 1994. *Now that I'm Married, Why Isn't Everything Perfect?* Boston: Little, Brown and Company.

Palmer, P. J. 1991. *The Active Life: Wisdom for Work, Creativity, and Caring*. San Francisco: HarperSanFrancisco.

Paul, S. C. 1992. *Inneractions*. San Francisco: HarperSanFrancisco.

Pelletier, K. R. 1994. *Sound Mind, Sound Body*. New York: Simon & Schuster.

Roush, D. 1984. "Rational-Emotive Therapy and Youth." *Personnel and Guidance Journal*, 62. 414-417.

Senge, P. M. 1990. *The Fifth Discipline*. New York: Currency Doubleday.

Seligman, M. E. P. 1994. *What You Can Change and What You Can't*. New York: Alfred. A. Knopf.

Shapiro, S. B. & Reiff, J. 1993. "A Framework for Reflective Inquiry on Practice: Beyond Intuition and Experience." *Psychological Reports*, 73. 1379-1394.

Ueland, B. 1993. *Strength to Your Sword Arm: Selected Writings.* Duluth, MN: Holy Cow! Press.

Watts, A. 1975. *Psychotherapy East and West.* New York: Vintage.

Welwood, J. 1990. *Journey of the Heart.* New York: HarperCollins.

Wheatley, M. J. 1992. *Leadership and the New Science.* San Francisco: Berrett-Koehler.

Wheelis, A. 1973. *How People Change.* New York: Harper & Row.

Wilber, K. 1985. *No Boundary.* Boston: Shambhala.

Witte, H. 1985. *Coping Effectively with Life.* Omaha, NE: University of Nebraska Medical Center.

Wolinsky, S. H. 1994. *The Tao of Chaos.* Bearsville, NY: Bramble Books.

Zukav, G. 1989. *The Seat of the Soul.* New York: Simon & Schuster.

ORDER FORM

Please send the following book:

Moving into Balance: Creating Your Personal Pathway
By Barbara Larrivee
ISBN 0-9651780-9-9 (pbk.), at $14.95 each

NAME _____

ADDRESS _____

CITY _____ STATE _____

ZIP _____ — _____

TELEPHONE (_____)_____

Shipping:
Priority mail: $3.00 for first copy; $1.50 each additional
Book Rate: $2.00 for first copy; $1.00 each additional

Quantity _____ x $14.95 each $ _____

Plus 8.25% tax for books shipped to California addresses   _____

SUBTOTAL   _____

Plus shipping (see note above)   _____

TOTAL Enclosed $ _____

Make payable to:

SHORELINE PUBLICATIONS
2118 Wilshire Boulevard, Suite 674
Santa Monica, CA 90403-5784

Trade discounts extended to book dealers, wholesalers, distributors.
Please contact (310) 450-2228 for information.